PIONEERS OF THE
CARIBBEAN

INGRID V LAMBIE & PATRICIA L TULLY

 FriesenPress

Suite 300 - 990 Fort St
Victoria, BC, V8V 3K2
Canada

www.friesenpress.com

Illustrations by Uche Uwadinachi

Front cover and Back cover designed by Uche Uwadinachi

Authors Photographs:
 1 Ingrid V Lambie by Ingrid V Lambie
 2 Patricia L Tully by Ann Granger - Ant.gua

ISBN
978-1-5255-8694-1 (Hardcover)
978-1-5255-8695-8 (Paperback)
978-1-5255-8696-5 (eBook)

1. BIOGRAPHY & AUTOBIOGRAPHY, PERSONAL MEMOIRS

Distributed to the trade by The Ingram Book Company

TABLE OF CONTENTS

|||||||||||||||||||||||||||||||||||||||||||||||||||||||||||||||||||||||||||||||||||||||||||||||||||||||

BOOK 2: VERONICA'S STORY   81

BOOK 1

||||||||||||||||||||||||||||||||||

DOLVIS STORY

||||||||||||||||||||||||||||||||||||||||||||||||||

Book 1 is dedicated to my mom Dolvis whose love, dedication and support are the cornerstone of her story and my life. Thank you, mom from the bottom of my heart for all the love you poured through me and in me and to all others who were lucky to be a part of your journey.

INTRODUCTION

Pioneers of the Caribbean is about real life experiences the struggles, family, culture-shock, setting and achieving goals. The stories have their genesis in the Caribbean with its warmth, beautiful scenery, and calm sea waters with white sand and blue skies. The African, Amerindian, Indian and European traditions, added a rich culture and flowery language. Artistry, rich music and culinary with great taste from the animals, vegetation and numerous different types of fruits found in the back yards and the marketplaces.

The strong resilient women that were driven, courageous, determined, dedicated and had a strong faith and a vision in mind. They ventured out into the unknown with a mind set to achieve their goals for their families in providing a better quality of life with good education to motivate their children to achieve. These women embraced the opportunities that were presented to them, they relocated their families and experienced culture shock and endured harsh winter weather in their migration to Canada.

Canada was a new and young country which had opened up their immigration and provided different schemes to attract tradesmen, skilled and non-skilled persons. This was great even with the many challenges and the sacrifices these mothers had to make including leaving their families behind and their young children to find hope in a new life.

They worked hard and saved to provide for their families and to bring them to Canada where everyone could get an education and work to assist each other in attaining the goals that were set so everyone could reach their full potential and find their purpose in life to make their contribution to society.

"In those days, some children went to school without shoes on their feet, determined to get an education."

"Mom kept small quantities of money in her possession, such as five-dollar bills; and she would put the money into the hands of family members, children and adults, including adopted members and their children."

"Ruth heart skipped a beat at the return of her grandchildren and even though she said nothing she didn't have a good feeling about Canada, and snow and its effects on the lives of her grandchildren. The next day however, the car was sent to pick up the girls and again after goodbyes Baba escorted his grandchildren to the airport and off to their new land."

"Noel was subsidizing his mistress and only providing funds for food and some utilities. Dolvis had bought the home and it was her responsible to cover mortgage and all other major bills.

Dolvis was determined and embarked on two different business ventures. The first was foster care of children. No doubt here she was encouraged and sought counsel from Annie. Annie was boarding children of West Indian parents but Dolvis decided to go another route by taking in foster children."

As you read about the different experiences of the families the emotions, the sense of pride, the anger, boredom, desire for home and old friends; the transient, negotiation, adjustment and adoption made through personal sacrifices. Honouring commitments and love of family to achieve goals; may you be enlightened and enjoy the journeys and be blessed for it.

WOMEN

They were not the Magi

They were not Men

They were not Three
They were Women

Who didn't find any star
To follow

Except their courage
Leading them

They met hurdles
They dared…Fought

Soon, Excelled

And found the Promise.

DOVES

Like Doves

They Drove

Across the clouds
And heights

They met Rain
And Thunderstorms

Soon became friends
With lightening and wind

They found trees soon

And birth Beautiful Birds

DO-VE DO lvis and VE ronica
Two brave Women of the Sky.

Poems by Uche Uwadinachi

CHAPTER I

||||||||||||||||||||||||||||||||||||||||||||||||||||||||||||

THE EARLY YEARS IN JAMAICA

Dolvis story began on a small island in the Caribbean known as Jamaica. Jamaica is the 3rd largest island in the Caribbean which for many years prospered under British rule or better stated the British empire prospered while owners of the island. Main export of the island up to the 1970's were bauxite and other agricultural products such as banana and sugar. Jamaicans in the latter 50's and early sixties were getting very disenchanted with British rule and the imbalance of the class system in Jamaica supported by their British landlord. Hence the people rebelled and petitioned for independence. As a result, on August 6th, 1962 Jamaica was declared an independent nation able to decide its own fate and the direction of the Jamaican people.

Two strong political parties formed the popular two opposing parties, the Labour Party led by Alexander Bustamante and the Peoples National Party led by Norman Manley. Both leaders even though different in ideology were blood cousins. Bustamante became the 1st prime minister of Jamaica after independence in August 1962.

I am however getting ahead of myself here and so will have to bring you back to the time of my mother's birth on June 30th, 1922. At that time Jamaica was still a colony under British rule. Consequently, Jamaica's culture and economics were controlled, influenced, and run by the British parliament. Whatever impacted the British empire impacted Jamaica and the Jamaican people. That included both World Wars servicemen were recruited from Jamaica and other islands controlled by the British The financial setback of the

7

great depression in the 1930's and the potato famine in the British empire all kept Jamaicans at a base level economically.

Jamaica is blessed with tropical warm weather and lush green fertile lands all year round. Most of the island's fertile ground provides food so that hunger has never been a major crisis in the island.

In the early 1900,s the Jamaican population was a mixture of British estate owners, the freed slaves of African descent, the biracial mixture of the Africans and British, the Chinese workers brought to Jamaica, and the South Asian brought to Jamaica to assist with farming. Other immigrant groups such as the Jews fleeing from persecution, Germans, Spanish and other immigrants helped to make Jamaica a melting pot. Hence the motto for independence "out of many one people."

Dolvis Melvina Lawrence came into the world to Ruth Ann Waisome a self-educated orphan who lost her mother at the age of 12. Her father James Waisome remarried shortly after and had 2 other daughters with his second wife before he died in his early 40's. Ruth was forced to be independent and had to find her own way in the world. The rumours were back then that her mother had been poisoned for land. Land was the great commodity for everyone in the early 1900's. Britain fought and died for land in the colonies. In Jamaica and most of the Caribbean islands the interbreeding of the slaves with the landowners had resulted in land being passed on to the bi-racial offsprings who now became landowners.

James Waisome was of black and Scottish descent and owned a lot of prime land in the parish of Westmoreland but Ruth didn't have the mind or desire to be a farmer. She wanted more out of life. Ruth yearned for the city life and the opportunity to see more of the world. Ruth was the older of the two and was outgoing and adventurous. Her younger sister Agnes was her constant companion and they formed a partnership selling goods in the markets of Kingston. Agnes was shy reserved and quiet but combined with the outgoing warm natured Ruth they were a dynamic duo.

Westmoreland was a very fertile parish and flourished with good crops such as bananas, yams tropical fruits such as mangoes guavas and vegetables. Ruth did very well as a higgler a term used for the market salesmen and women. They would travel from the countryside with their produce and take trains, buses or whatever transport available to bring them to the city to sell their goods. You could see them loading up their produce in big straw baskets crocheted into a tight intricate weave to provide strength and durability. They would then balance on their heads to bring into their destinations in the marketplace.

The marketplace was a thriving busy place of different smells, from the sweet fragrance of tropical fruits such as mangoes, oranges, and sweet sop to the musky smells of the ground provisions such as yams and breadfruit. Close by the fish mongerers goods would fill the air with the smells of the seas and a vast array of colourful fishes would be on display such as parrot, snapper, goatfish and grouper.

As a child I loved going to market with my granny as Ruth was called by her grandchildren. The smells of the marketplace always provided a warm comforting buzz and my eyes would dart around trying to take in all the sights and sounds. The sellers would be adored in colourful gingham printed garments with full aprons to keep their clothing clean and intact. The higglers would be calling to all the patrons coming into the market in a sing song fashion. One such phrase they would call out to me was "come ya pretty gal cum and try me ripe banana."

Granny Ruth was a buxom lady with beautiful cocoa butter skin, strong shapely legs and a warm smile full of personality and charm. She had gold caps on the edges of her front teeth as full gold would have been too crude and common. She was a woman of breeding and character and always dressed well with style and grace. The other higglers were always happy to see her and even though they tried to charm me to get her to buy; she had a keen business sense and knew how to haggle for the bottom line. I was always amazed at how Ruth and the other higglers could add multiply and subtract in less than 10 seconds in their heads. They were no calculators back then. Math was an essential tool for survival. Granny Ruth did not finish public school and neither did any of the other sellers in the market, but they could add, subtract, multiply and divide in a matter of seconds. Each of them carried a money pouch on the side of their garments ready to give change and move on to the next customer.

It was during her travels to Kingston that Ruth met Mr Lawrence a businessman. Mr Lawrence was a successful highly respected businessman well-dressed dark-skinned, short in stature and of slim build. Ruth was attracted to his success and his years of formal schooling. Ruth was also very conscious of the colour biases in Jamaica at that time. She took great pride in her darker skin tone and had a preference for the darker skinned man. Ruth Ann fell for his charm and so it was that on June 30th, 1922 she gave birth to Dolvis Melvina Lawrence, her only child. Unfortunate for Ruth Mr. Lawrence chose to marry one much fairer than Ruth as was the practice back then for successful black men to marry mulatto women. It was the ultimate sign of status and prestige and solidified they had now arrived in society.

Slavery and slave owners had left a tarnished and distorted view of colour on the Caribbean culture; hence the lighter skin women and men were highly valued. This was a major blow to Ruth an independent woman who had earned her way in society but was still discarded by a black man because like him she had darker skin. Ruth was now a single mother whose sole purpose was to raise her dark-skinned daughter with the purpose and goal of getting an education. Her daughter was going to have the best education, something she was deprived off due to the early death of her mother.

Dolvis birth in the early 1920's in the time known as the roaring 20's were good times for Britain after winning the 1st world war. Britain owned most of the new world countries which included Jamaica and most of the Caribbean. The marketplace was thriving, and so Ruth was able to support her only child. She also was now travelling to other islands such as British Honduras to buy and sell goods. It was on one such excursion that Ruth met her husband, life partner and love of her life Albert White; a mulatto of Scottish and black descent. Albert was dark-skinned with the same cocoa complexion of Ruth. He was a serious businessman with straight black hair and straight features. Albert was also an immaculate dresser a trait important to Ruth and her need for social graces and flawless appearance. Ruth had been severely burned by Mr. Lawrence so she was very hard on Albert and refused to marry him even though he proposed within the 1st year of meeting Ruth. It was after 6 years of courtship, living and partnering together that Ruth finally conceded. She felt he had proven himself to be worthy of her and her daughter's love and affection. This fact Albert himself proudly repeated in their 35th year wedding anniversary celebrations. Their marriage he further stated was a marriage based on love, hard work, dedication and trust. Albert was delighted to have Ruth and Dolvis as his family. He proved to be a doting father for Dolvis as well. He was diabetic and as a result Ruth was never able to conceive another child. All efforts were then focused on Dolvis and her schooling.

Dolvis had half-brothers and sisters by her father who were exceptional students and in whom he had made extensive educational investments. They were all educated abroad and became professionals in various fields such as lawyers, engineers, and professors. Ruth was very competitive as well and this fact must have propelled her on to ensure that her child out of wedlock was not a failure and could stand toe to toe with her successful half brothers and sisters.

Dolvis was blessed from an early age with two loving and devoted parents. Ruth had chosen wisely and carefully for a husband. She had learned from her past mistakes. Albert and Ruth continued to work together to improve their status into middle class society.

Jamaica and Jamaicans had evolved with a British mindset and this was evident in the prevailing class biases. So much so that it was devastating to a family for a son or daughter to marry across classes. Even though education was the best way for a poor family to bring themselves out of poverty there was still the sting of the poor family background that would keep him or her out of the right job or social circles.

Ruth and Albert through hard work and discipline managed to buy their first home in the city in the mid 40's. They were able to open it up as a boarding house and rent out rooms to enable them to pay off the mortgage. This was a viable and growing business. The growth in industry in the city of Kingston resulted in a lot of families who were farmers now migrating to the city to fill jobs in manufacturing or sending their kids to learn trades in the city. Most newcomers to the city were happy to rent a room where they would share kitchen and bathroom at a weekly or monthly rate.

Electricity was not yet a popular commodity in the 1940's and coal was the most commonly used means of cooking and heating. Most of the tenants would use a coal stove and then buy coal to use for cooking. A kitchen was not necessary as these coal stoves could be set up outside. The food cooked by those means had a great flavor with a hint of coal. As a child I enjoyed my granny's potato pudding which was cooked on the coal stove. The potato pudding is a baked dish combined with sweet potato, coconut milk, sugar and spices. Granny Ruth had a way of placing the coals on the bottom of the pot and on the top of the pot. The very smell of the sweetened coconut was heaven.

It was a twelve-hour ritual of slow baking on the coal stove but at the end of the day the sweet soft coconut flavoured dish was worth its' weight in gold.

Railways were the most common source of transporting goods at that time. Bauxite one of Jamaica's main export was discovered in the 1940's making railway travel that more important to move goods and people. This also created migration of more people from the country areas to the city of Kingston to find manufacturing jobs. The railway was however impacted by two traumatic incidents in the 1950's one being Hurricane Charlie which damaged the infra-structure in 1951 and Kendall Crash on September 1st, 1957. There were 1600 passengers on board and the derailment of the train resulted in 175 deaths and over 800 passengers injured. My cousin Ivy vividly remembers this crash as she lost a few friends and was spared because my granny Ruth refused to let her go on the train trip with her friends.

Ruth was a stern disciplinarian and everyone who knew her can attest to that characteristic. Her only daughter Dolvis was also not immune to her discipline. Dolvis was a very obedient and studious child. Ruth had big dreams for her only daughter. Most ambitious girls in the 1940's in the Caribbean had two options to be a teacher or a nurse. Dolvis had a caring heart and decided to study nursing. Dolvis as her name implied was a beautiful young lady. She had the same cocoa-coloured perfect skin as her mother Ruth but was shorter and petite with straight features and thin lips. Dolvis beauty is best depicted in a poem by Nigerian poet Uche Uwadinachi.

> Babe, what it is
> About you
> That photographers
> Crave for?
>
> Your eyes?
> Warm, pretty translucent lamps
> Staring like low current bulbs
> In Mofuloku streets.
>
> Nne biko, your eyes
> Are cyberstalking me!
> Your shoulders blade?
> Proud like the wings of an airplane

On the runway
Of Lagos-Ibadan
Please, can you
Be my National Carrier?

Perhaps, it's your strut,
Smart aerobics
Intimidating the world
With its swift heels,
I wish this was why Vat was
Inflated
I would not complain

Tell me your secret
Name your price?
I can pay with more loans
From the World Bank
And also secure you a space
At the United Nations photoshoot
Only if you tell me
Why you are so gorgeous!

Poem by Uche Uwadinachi

Yes, that poem could have been written for either women as Dolvis had inherited Ruth's great looks and both were stunningly beautiful black women.

Ruth was vivacious but Dolvis was naturally reserved with a shyness that some might interpret for coldness. This might have been the result of the careful, protective manner she was nurtured by her mother Ruth. Ruth loved her daughter dearly and wanted the best for her and that included an easier path without all the bumps she had to endure to make life.

Dolvis had a smooth transition into her 20's completing her nursing career; however, 1940's Jamaica still had the same cultural biases that did not escape Ruth in the 1920's. Dolvis met her nemesis in Mr. Barrett and gave birth to her first daughter Joy in March of 1944. Dolvis and Joy never saw or heard from Mr. Barrett again. Dolvis rejection was two-fold not only from the father of her child but also her mother. Ruth was so disappointed in her daughter that she was forced to leave home and fend for herself. Dolvis was able to weather the storm and continue her career path, Ruth did come to terms and grew to love and support her daughter and granddaughter. She did this as Dolvis persevered and proceeded on her career path despite her error in judgement. So much so that Joy was jointly raised by Dolvis and her grandparents Ruth and Albert or Baba as he was fondly called by all the grandkids. Joy fondly remembers all the love showered on her by her grandparents and how much time they took to nurture and spend with her.

Ruth and Albert were now proud owners of their second home at 22 ½ Cambridge Street Franklin Town in east Kingston. This was an upper middle-class community and they were proud of their struggles and accomplishments. With less economic stress they were more relaxed in their parenting styles and could spoil their granddaughter. Dolvis career as a maternity and public health nurse took her all over the island. She got the opportunity to work on the estate homes in Portland. Joy fondly remembers the beautiful estate homes and lush scenery of Portland. Ruth herself had a health setback which now meant she had to give up selling in the market. Albert started a grocery store business in Clarendon which kept him away most of the week and he would return home on weekends. Ruth loved company so her granddaughter Joy was that needed company as well as her niece Ivy who was the daughter of her sister and partner Agnes. Agnes had now also retired from the marketplace and was busy managing the family home in Westmoreland with her eldest sister Mary.

Education was still the main pursuit for Dolvis who continued her professional work which included travelling from one end of the island to the other. It was during this time she met her final charmer, my dad Noel Benjamin Lambie. Noel was a widow who had lost his first wife to breast cancer and had been left with 6 children the youngest child my sister Lelieth just 6 months old. Hence the need to find another wife and mother as soon as was respectable. Noel had moved his mother Claudia into the family home in St Mary to assist with taking care of his children.

Noel was a tall light skinned, full faced man with curly black hair and a warm playful smile. I can see why my mom found him irresistible. He had a friendly outgoing personality while she was reserved. He also owned a motorcycle which was only available to those who had some means in the 1950's. He was hot and on wheels!!!

After a two-year courtship and the expected arrival of my sister Charmaine, Noel and Dolvis were married in May 1953 in a quiet afternoon ceremony. Noel needed a caregiver for his children and as much as he cared for Dolvis, Noel was a practical man and recognized that her skills as a nurse was a great asset for him and his children. Noel had primary school education and was one of seven children for Claudia and Mr. Lambie. Mr. Lambie had died early leaving Claudia to fend for herself and her seven children. Both Claudia and Mr. Lambie were bi-racial of Scottish and black parentage. The Lambies' were prominent estate holders who hailed from Scotland hence Noel had inherited the family farm of some 60 plus acres. This he managed with the help of farm-workers as he was not a natural farmer. He had held a government job prior to meeting Dolvis which he acquired with the help of his brother Sydney who was a popular Member of Parliament for the St Ann parish area.

Noel, however; was an independent thinking man who preferred the freedom of being self-employed so was quite happy managing the farm. He also had learned the trade of a tailor. Noel was street smart and not book smart hence he was sent to learn a trade. Tailoring was one of the soft trades and Noel did not care much for hard labour. Noel proceeded to set up a tailor shop in front of the farmhouse so that he could also run his tailoring business from home.

The main crop of the farm was bananas and I can recall as a child the farm-workers cutting down the many fingers of banana and lying them out waiting for the trucks to pick up and deliver for market. The greenery of the bananas created a lush landscape as far as the eyes could see.

Bananas were a main agricultural crop as it was a staple food eaten both green and ripe by every Jamaican family. The green banana is loaded with iron and when boiled in the morning with ackee and saltfish as was the practice especially on a Sunday morning, provided most families with a brunch style breakfast. That same banana was also grated and put in a porridge for the family with condensed milk and spices. Finally, the banana was eaten like the rest of the world ripe and sweet as a fruit. There were so many different bananas on the farm, and each had its own taste, look and feel. My favourite was the short fat midget bananas as they had a sweet almost honey-like taste that is hard to find in supermarkets today. Other fruits such as coconuts, guava, mangoes of all variety were also plentiful on the farm.

As a child my fondest memories was hiking on the farm. My sisters and I would set out early after breakfast and with cutlass in hand travel through the farm eating whatever fruit we fancied. On the menu was always coconut water and jelly to ease us from the heat and allow us to proceed on our journey. One such voyage did result in a mishap for my sister Charmaine, while trying to cut into the coconut she also cut off a piece of her finger. My older sisters ran all the way home crying knowing there would be trouble as they allowed Charmaine who was much younger to use the cutlass. I do believe that helped to propel my sister Liz to become a nurse as she was most empathetic to Charmaine's plight. The finger did grow back and was hardly noticeable to the eye, but we also learned from the elders that it was important to have kept the finger warm, so that it could be sewn back on instead of given into panic and tears. Indeed, many life lessons were learned on the farm.

Noel was a proud and respected man in his community. He was considered upper middle class in Wood Park, St Mary. He had a farm and a tailor shop. His mother Claudia was fortunate to have had a son who was a casualty of the 2nd World War; as a result, she received a pension from his brave duty serving in the British army. Most of the other farmers in the community were not so fortunate. They were workers on the farm who made a small stipend and would also take food from the farm to their homes to feed their families. Most of their children did not attend school and those that did went to school without shoes.

Charmaine was born in July 1953 two months after their marriage. Dolvis continued to pursue her nursing career and was posted in Mandeville soon after Charmaine's birth. She was now the mother of two natural children and six stepchildren. Her income now had to be sourced out to assist her husband with the needs of his children. Such things as clothing and schooling were of prime consideration. Food was not of prime concern as Noel had the farm with built in provisions for the home.

Dolvis continued to focus on her career but she could see difficult times ahead especially when it came to education for the rather large family. This was of prime importance to both my parents and at that time in the island higher education was only free to those who were smart enough to pass an island wide exam. Both Noel and Dolvis were doing a lot of commuting in the early years of marriage and juggling the extended family. Some of Noel's younger children would come and spend time with their stepmom in Manchester. One of the middle children Dorothy spend a lot of time there as Dolvis found her to be a very bright and well behaved child. She also was quite a pretty young girl with fair skin and brown wavy hair. It was during this time that Dolvis became pregnant with her second child less than a year after having Charmaine. Noel was proving to be a very fertile man. Noel was 9 year older than Dolvis who was now thirty-two years old and becoming a mother for the third time. I was born in the fall on November 23rd, 1954 and named Ingrid after the actress Ingrid Bergman. Dolvis needed a little movie fantasy to get her out of her present-day reality of motherhood with 9 children and now 11 mouths to feed.

Her first daughter Joy was having her own issues adjusting to all these extra mouths to feed and a stepfather who did not have time or energy to bond with a child that was not his own. Ruth was also having grave concerns about the enormous burden that her only daughter had now taken upon herself. This was not the easy life route that she had envisioned for her only child.

She was not a happy mother in law as she could see a rough road ahead for her daughter and her choices. Dolvis had worked right up to the time she gave birth to me and I was a difficult child who would not be weaned. Dolvis had to return to work promptly so she had to turn again to her mother Ruth in Kingston for help and sent me as a young baby just a year old to her mother to assist with the weaning. I was assisted on the journey by Ivy her niece and godchild. This relief was short lived as Dolvis became pregnant once again within two years with Sharon their final child born in September 1956. By then Dolvis had relocated to Kingston and was staying in her mother's home. Sharon was born at home and the count continues. There was now a total of 10 children to feed, clothes and send to school.

It was in the spring of 1957 when my sister Sharon was barely a year old Dolvis decided to pursue further studies in the United States of America. A new profession was on the horizon in the field of diets and that sparked an interest in her. She enjoyed cooking and was also an excellent baker especially of Jamaican rum cakes which she tiredly worked hard at perfecting her skills. Rum cakes are a stable to the Jamaican culture, it is felt that it might have been inspired by the Portuguese who came to Jamaica and introduced their fruit cakes. The Jamaican twist of these cakes however include soaking of all dried fruits available such as raisins, currants and prunes in wine and rum for up to a year, so the fruits are fully absorbed and blended with the liquor. Then flour butter sugar and eggs are added to this fruit liquor mixture and baked to produce a mouthwatering cake loaded with liquor. If not careful one could be drunk for many days. The cake is normally served in small slices on special events such as weddings and Christmas dinners. With a firm sight on her dreams and knowing that her mother Ruth was fully capable of taking care of her daughters Dolvis was on her way.

Ruth was estatic and encouraged Dolvis to study in the United States. Dolvis was having a difficult life with all the additional stepchildren and her income as a nurse could only stretch so far. This was also a degree program from one of the universities in New York. Dolvis would also be staying with her half-sister Vivian who had also been living and studied in New York and already has a master's Degree in English. Mom was an excellent student and looking forward to the experience. Noel, however; was not in favour of his wife travelling so far away. He was not a man who could cope well with a long separation and he also did not know what to expect from the men in a foreign land. Would they be inclined to make a pass on his wife? This he did not have a clue.

So, it was in the fall of 1957 Dolvis embarked on her journey to the USA. Life in the USA was a wonderful and positive experience for Dolvis. New York was a fast and vibrant city with so much to do and learn. Dolvis was energized by the experience and the people. Her sister Viv as she was called was excited to have her. Dolvis settled easily into in her new life and pursuit of higher education. Viv had also married a professor and had no children. She also made the offer to Dolvis to take care of one of her girls. She was my godmother and would be happy to help raise and nurture my education. Noel was a proud dad and was not inclined to farm out any of his children regardless of how difficult finances were at the time. Dolvis's social life took flight in the Big Apple as she met modern American black women who smoked, partied, and enjoyed their life. One of her best friends was a lady name Cynthia who was light skinned with a beautiful built like Dorothy Dandridge. She was also outgoing and knew all the hot spots. She loved to party and enjoyed drinking and smoking. Dolvis was introduced to all the best hair products, fashion and hair styles through Cynthia's influence. Mom learned to balance her time between schoolwork, studying and odd jobs from nanny care to cleaning, New York Style which was drinking coffee and minimal sleep. Mom was not a drinker or smoker but to the end was a coffee drinker which she would have at least twice daily to keep her going. She successfully achieved her goal of becoming a qualified dietician with a degree in dietetics and returned to Jamaica in 1960. I can still recall her re-entry into Jamaica in 1960 and the transformation of my mom into a modern American fashion model. Her hair was long and beautifully straightened in a page boy style hanging down her back. She was wearing pedal pushers which was one of the big fashion trends in the late 50's and to complete the look was the high heeled pointed toe pumps. I did not recognize this beauty at first until she came up to me, gave me hug and presented me with a walking doll much bigger than myself another must have toy for the child back then. Yes, mom had visited and conquered the American way of life and was ready to display her gifts and await reentry.

With her new skills she landed an excellent job at one of the major hospitals in Kingston. She now settled back into life in Jamaica with dreams of returning to America. Dolvis had tasted life outside of Jamaica and had seen the possibilities in the foreign land of United States of America. She knew it would offer her and her family a much better life and greater opportunities.

Studying abroad had also presented many challenges for her. Money earned abroad was used to send back to Jamaica to assist her mother with paying for care for her daughters. Her marriage to Noel also had a downside, he was not in alignment with her need to study much less to study in another country; furthermore, he had taken on a mistress while she was away. Dolvis, however; had to keep her focus and her eye on the goal and not let his actions deter her or prevent her from what was most important for the family. She had her children to focus on and the dream of returning to America so that her children could have a better life and more opportunities for learning.

Early pic of myself and older sister Charmaine. It was the practice back then to go to the photo studio and have family pics taken of the family. Charmaine was always smiling as she was a happy outgoing child and loved rag dolls also a rave back then. Those dresses were local dresses most likely made by a dressmaker. All children were also not considered dressed until hair was done up with ribbons.

This pic was me and my younger and baby of the family Sharon. Also done at photo studio. I was holding doll my mom had brought back from USA as my gift. I believe it was the walking doll which was the rave back then. Dresses were also from USA.

CHAPTER 2

||||||||||||||||||||||||||||||||||||||||||||||||||||||||||||||||

VOYAGE TO A NEW LAND!!

Almost 3 years had passed since her return to Jamaica and no word from the American Embassy approving travel for her and her family. It was in passing that a fellow worker suggested to her that Canada was expanding and looking for professionals to come to their country. She had little or no information about Canada but time was running out, so she went and applied to the Canadian Embassy. Much to her amazement she was accepted and without further ado she was on her way to Canada in early September 1963.

As it so happens her cousin Mrs. Baxter and her husband also made the trip to Canada earlier in the year and they needed someone to bring their two children Una and Tanny to Canada. She was happy to oblige as it meant she was not traveling alone. She also now had somewhere to stay until she found employment and got settled elsewhere. Job hunting went very well as within the first month with her strong newly acquired skills as a dietician she was fortunate to get a job working as a food supervisor at Scarborough General Hospital in Scarborough. Her focus was now on the next goal of saving and bringing up the rest of the family. Dolvis was an excellent worker with strong managerial skills, very diplomatic and worked very well with people. So much so that she would often go the extra mile to assist them in times of need.

She was having a personal battle of her own in her husband Noel's defiance against coming to Canada. Noel was still openly living with a mistress in Jamaica and she knew that as a single parent bringing up four girls would be extremely difficult. She was at a crossroad. It was at this point she was walking along Kennedy Road in Scarborough and came across a Nazarene Church. Religion had never been a prime focus in her life, but she felt a pull that day to enter and just pour out her concerns to a higher force. She had grown up and gone to church and had a belief in God, but Ruth had not forced her to attend church; school and her career had always been the goal. She had been privy to the Pocomania churches in Jamaica as well that believed in the rituals of getting rid of evil spirits. She had also taken time out to visit the so-called spiritual women in Jamaica, who would pray and offer remedies when you were feeling stress. After much debate she decided that this was more that she could manage on her own power, so this was worth a try. The church and its teachings were exactly what she needed. Dolvis felt a resurgent of her spirit and the inner strength to endure through her conversion and belief in God and the resurrected Christ. She also got baptized and received two of the gifting of the holy spirit which was the ability to speak in tongues and prayer. She would combine the two gifting in her prayer life with family and friends. The Nazarene church did not belief in the speaking of tongues so that gift she could not demonstrate or use at her home church.

The pastor Rev. Ronald Fry and his wife Elizabeth were also a built-in treasure of support and good will for her. They hailed from the Southern States and had that same southern gift of hospitality and home-grown warmth as her family life with Ruth and Albert. They had two beautiful children a young son and daughter. Both children were fair with soft blond curls and full of energy. The little girl reminded her of Shirley Temple from the movies with the same mischievous smile and boundless energy. Dolvis loved the movies and Shirley Temple was one of the popular actresses she had always loved on screen from her early days watching movies at Ward Theatre in Kingston. This loving warm family setting was what she needed until she could be reunited with her own family. She felt at peace!!

With Noel still on the fence she decided to sponsor her daughter Joy as she would soon be twenty-one. Dolvis knew that Joy could not be sponsored as easily after she was an adult. Joy had studied clerical and administrative skills in Jamaica and with her strong office skills would easily find a job and be able to assist with saving funds for the rest of the family to join them later.

The bond between mother and daughter was strengthened as they both worked and saved so that the other family members could join them in Canada as soon as finances would allow.

The following year in 1965 Keith Lambie the only boy in the family, son of Noel and stepson of Dolvis also joined Joy and Dolvis. Keith had tried his hand at several trade apprentice programs in Jamaica but was not strongly akin to any. He was the only boy in the family and Noel had always favoured his daughters. Noel was always fearful of boys and the dangers of them aligning with the wrong crowd, especially when they had no defined skills or purpose. Dolvis was happy to have Keith join her and Joy as she had not been fortunate to have a son of her own and felt a real kinship with her stepson. She managed to find Keith a job at the hospital working as a porter, hence plans for the rest of the family were full steam ahead. Dolvis, Joy and Keith formed the perfect team. All three were loyal and reliable worker bees focused on the goal of working, sharing and building the financial assets towards the end goal of all family members coming to Canada.

Finally, Noel started to realize the importance of bringing the family to Canada for better opportunity and education. Only one of his oldest daughters had passed full scholarship and it was looking bleak financially to pay to send seven girls to school if the younger ones also struggled with the island wise exam.

So it was that on Feb 28th, 1966 Noel and four of his daughters Dorothy, Liz, Lelieth and Charmaine boarded the plane for Canada. In preparation for this rather financial extravagant excursion from Jamaica Noel had to sell the family farm of some 66 acres at a time when no major profits were to made in selling that amount of land. Funds were needed to assist with settling the large family into Canada. Dolvis on the other side of the globe had to rent and furnish a much larger home to facilitate the family size. Yet, another surprise awaited them when the family arrived in Canada. The landed papers had also included the two smaller underage children, Sharon and I. Dolvis and Noel had planned to have the younger children stay a while longer with Ruth as they were doing well and both of them had felt it best to start with the older children, get them settled and then send for the younger two girls. They were however advised by immigration that the landed status would become void in a year and they would have to re-apply again for the younger children.

Faced with that daunting prospect they had no choice but to hurriedly revisit their budget and use funds slated for resettling into getting two more plane tickets for their new homeland.

The two younger children myself and my sister Sharon were now faced with receiving the dreaded telegram from abroad advising Ruth of the need to make an urgent trip alone to a new home in a foreign land.

Ruth had bonded greatly with her two younger grandchildren having taken care of them from they were babies. Sharon the youngest had been born at home and Dolvis first trip to America was taken when Sharon was just a year old. I was three but Ruth had been taken care of me from the age of one. Dolvis had been working in several parishes after my birth of and had sent me to stay with her grandmother sometime after my first birthday to focus on career goals.

The extended family was the norm in Jamaica and grandparents played a pivotal role in the care and upbringing of their grandchildren. Ruth was therefore greatly distressed at the thought of losing her grandchildren with so little warning. With much ado, however; she began the treacherous task of getting her two smaller charges ready for their arduous trip to their new land.

Ruth White was beside herself with last minute preparations sending her two grandchildren off to an unknown and cold land. It was February 28th, 1966. I had recently taken the common entrance exam and Ruth knew for certain I would pass as I had always not only been a bright child but had spent months preparing with all the necessary classes and extra tutoring for the exam. This exam was not taken lightly as it was the free ticket to high school and failure meant that you would be subjected to a trade or apprenticeship program or even worse the end of your formal education. The questions and exam itself were formed in England and even though Jamaica was now an independent nation the educational curriculum tests and evaluation was still based on the British model. Ruth was looking forward to the results and even more so to seeing her grandchild in a uniform at some highly acclaimed school in New Kingston. I had applied to two of my favourite schools based on their record of excellence and the smart and dignified school uniforms I admired passing by my gate. One was Excelsior and the second was St Andrew High. All school children in Jamaica wore uniforms and took great pride in their uniforms.

My current primary school Franklin Town Primary School also had a first-class reputation due to the headmistress Mrs. Hanshaw known for her proficiency in the art of teaching and discipline. Our colors were navy blue skirt, white blouse with a navy-blue tie with red stripes. I remember even though I was an exceptional student she gave me the strap as I made an ignorant comment about a very buxom girl in my class suggesting that having a boyfriend had caused her ample breasts. Mrs. Hanshaw was a no-nonsense headmistress and no vulgarity or implied vulgarity was tolerated in her school. I learned that day that she was partial to no one and her rules governed that school to keep and maintain order and the reputation of excellence.

Ruth needed more time, but she had only two weeks to pack and get her two granddaughters ready for their arduous travel to an unknown land and to parents who had become strangers.

Sharon my younger sister had been petted and coddled by Ruth so much so that if anyone had upset her during the day while Ruth was away, she would on clue start to cry all over on Ruth's return knowing that Ruth would reprimand the offender and reward her with candy.

Dolvis had spent a total of six years abroad. Three years studying in the States and three years in Canada upstarting her career in preparation for her family. Sharon was now nine years old and I was eleven. Ruth and Albert had been our full-time parents for most of our childhood. Noel lived and managed the farm in the country and even though we had spent summers there, we had not bonded with our father.

Time in the country was spent with our older half siblings and paternal grandmother Claudia Lambie fondly called Muma by all of her grandchildren. Claudia was also a kind spiritual soul who pampered all her grandchildren but had a special bond as well with my two youngest half-sisters Joy and Lelieth. This was because they were only a year and six months old when they had lost their mother to cancer. Claudia had been forced to step in as mother at that time to her six grandchildren. Claudia in contrast to Ruth was slim and fair with long straight hair due to her mulatto heritage of black and English. She had an even temperament and rarely got angry and was equally warm to all her grandchildren. She was a devout Christian and made sure all her grandchildren attended the small evangelical church just across from the family farm. She was the proud mother of six children Leila, Philip, Sydney, Noel my dad,

Gladys, and Edward. Edward my most dapper and handsome uncle had died as a war hero and the income received for his war service was the main source of income for Claudia. My grandfather had died early in the marriage and very little was ever said about him growing up. Philip had left Jamaica for the States where he later married an American and fathered one child Patricia.

Sydney had done well for himself and Claudia was very proud of his accomplishments. Sydney had entered the political arena and was the MP of the parish of St Ann. He had married a teacher and had four legitimate children Max, Leroy, Sonia, and Louis. Sydney did have two children prior to his marriage Una and Carmen and was rumoured to have at least three more children outside of the marriage. Sydney like my father was a looker and a charmer. They were even rumours that a famous singer from the island Millicent Small might be his child. She had a wonderful melodious voice and was popular for the pioneer breaking song "My Boy Lollipop".

Unfortunately, a year before I immigrated my uncle Sydney and his wife suffered a tragic end. He died suddenly from unknown causes and within two weeks after his death his wife was killed in a car accident when the brakes from her car failed while driving down a steep hill in St Ann. As a child I can remember all the superstitions and rumours surrounding that tragedy. Jamaicans are prone to superstitions and the popular belief was that Sydney had come to take his wife home. Because of their popularity in the region of St Ann their tragedy was front page news in the paper. Ruth made sure I was privy to the media drama and cut out the story in the papers for us to read. We were too young to make the trip for the state funeral they received as prominent members of the political parties at that time.

Ruth had no time to waste. Her grandchildren needed to be on a plane on March 12th and she had many things to do. These included packing, washing, and getting some of our favourite foods ready to go with us on their voyage. Fried fish, breadfruit, mangoes, pears, and any other fruit in season would ensure that her grandchildren would have foods that were familiar to eat. They had always been picky eaters and were skinny and small for their age and she had always taken special care in feeding them. Such foods as fresh cows' milk, milo, Ovaltine, and Horlicks were standard items on her grandchildren diet. Cod liver oil was always given as a daily supplement and of course their yearly herbal treatment to cleanse the colon and intestines of any impurities worms and build up. She was sure that she was sending her grandchildren strong and healthy to their parents. Her job was complete, and she was happy and content that she was able to help. She still had another grandniece at home to care for her as Pauline was still waiting on her mom Mavis in England to send for her. She was happy to still have some company at home.

March 12th, 1966 arrived sooner than she would have liked, and it was a beautiful day in Jamaica, sunny and warm. Baba was taking us to the airport as Ruth could not bear to have to say goodbye to us at the airport. A taxi was reserved for the trip and after hugs and kisses Ruth waved a final goodbye to her granddaughters.

We were off to an unknown land in a big bird in the sky called a plane to reunite with parents and siblings that had now become strangers. Fate intervened however, on this first attempt at flight as there was a major snowstorm in Canada causing us to return home to await another attempt the next day if the weather improved.

Ruth heart skipped a beat at the return of her grandchildren and even though she said nothing she did not have a good feeling about Canada, snow and its effects on the lives of her grandchildren. The next day however, the car was sent to pick up the girls and again after goodbyes Baba escorted his grandchildren to the airport and off to their new land.

Sharon and I were off travelling on a plane to unimagined adventures. I was older and very inquisitive by nature, so my eyes were peeled to everything that was happening around me. The airport with all the people in uniforms and the chatter and noise of the big bird like objects coming to land was exciting and scary at the same time. How did that massive thing stay up in the sky was something I had not yet learned in school. My mind was racing with excitement and wonder. The stewardess as the lady on the plane was called was extremely attentive to Sharon and me. She did her best to make us comfortable and safe. Looking out the window as the plane ascended into the clouds was strange and somewhat discomforting for me. My ears were also extremely sensitive to the noise and the plane taking on more altitude. I could feel no sound and then a pop sound in my ear as sound returned. This was a strange experience for us both. Sharon who had been babied and pampered was content to just sleep. The complimentary meal was an out of body experience; the bland tasting vegetables and white coloured chicken with no browning sauce or pepper was foreign and distasteful to our palate. We feasted mostly on the sugar filled dessert and juice drinks given to us as we were sure there would be a meal waiting for us at home that would be more inviting to our palate. We were most curious to see where this big bird would land and what path our life would take in this new strange land.

Our first shock was the feeling of cold as we landed and walked into the airport from the plane. This was a new experience not well received by both of us. Ruth had given us a merino and sweater to wear but we had never experienced this kind of cold that was piercing through every fibre of our being. This feeling was further intensified by all the strange looking people that we now encountered, all were fair skinned with straight hair and a funny accent. They were also wearing heavy outer garments and high shoes that came up almost to their knees As a child we were told it was bad manners to stare at people but I felt like everything and everyone around me was not real and since I was dreaming then it was ok.

Our stewardess was very attentive and helpful and brought us through the airport and into a seated area with two of the fair skinned men where we were told to have a seat and they would check our documents and let our parents know that we had arrived.

Unfortunately, we failed to have one important document and that was the landed slip. Dolvis was a pioneer and the ground breaker in getting our family out of Jamaica but she was the only working parent when we arrived in Canada and she could not take time off again to meet us at the airport

It was after some time my father had to be summoned to meet us in immigration. It was good for us to finally see a familiar face. Noel at this point had only been in the country 2 weeks and here he was being questioned about his two younger children and why we were travelling without proper entry documents. At this point I thought for sure that my sister and I were destined to be put on the next plane back to Jamaica; however, my father with his strong social skills saved the day. He started a personal conversation with the officers on his cultural Scottish and black heritage and life as a farmer. He became their immediate friend and so they were proud to welcome him and his family to Canada. Our passports were then stamped and Noel Lambie and his family were wished a happy life and welcome to their new land. This was my first lesson in networking in Canada. Noel was a farmer and businessman and was used to forming alliances in order to get the job done. This was what he did best. It was obvious that he had now come on page with my mom with his skills and determination both were intent on making the transition to their new home and new country a success.

CHAPTER 3

||||||||||||||||||||||||||||||||||||||||||||||||||||||||||||||

LIFE IN CANADA-
GETTING SETTLED!!

Dolvis was a tenacious leader, teacher, and pioneer. Her dream had now landed us all in Canada. This was now the beginning of a new life in a new land. Our new home was a semi-detached five-bedroom home in the suburbs of Agincourt. We were lucky to have five adults working but with an additional seven mouths to feed it was essential for Noel to find a job.

Dolvis with her new-found belief in God made it an essential component of our Sunday life to get to church on Sundays. The chosen church was Kennedy Rd Church of the Nazarene. Reverend Fry and his wife Elizabeth were warm and personable with 2 beautiful fair-haired children. They hailed from the Southern United States and lived on the church property. Mrs. Fry had a knack for dressing well and looking great. She took great pride in coordinating her children's clothing as well as her own outfits with matching purses and elaborate hats. She also got my older siblings involved in organizing fashion shows at the church. She was not the best homemaker or cook. Reverend Fry loved and encouraged my mother's culinary skills so much so that Dolvis who enjoyed singing but could not carry a tune was allowed to sing solos anytime her heart desired. I remember as a teenage trying to avoid the service where my mom was scheduled for her solo performance. No matter how we tried to dissuade her from inflicting embarrassment on the family she continued to subject us to that ritual form of musical punishment. Her love of music did not stop there, she tried desperately to give us piano lessons taught by the church pianist Carol. After becoming disappointed in our lack of interest Dolvis decided the piano was there and she loved music, so she traded in the piano, got an organ, and enrolled in music lessons herself. I remember the torture of having to listen to her practice on weekends playing the organ and singing for her Sunday solo!!

Dolvis excelled at multitasking and finding ways to bring it extra income for the family. The family shared in the financial expense of running a home. Her main job was a dietitian at Scarborough General Hospital but that income alone could not feed a family of 10. My oldest siblings Keith and Joy had full-time jobs and they were required to assist with the financial burden by paying room and board with each pay. My dad Noel was 51 when he immigrated to Canada and he had been managing the family farm for the latter part of the years before he immigrated. He also had a side trade as a tailor while in Jamaica. His tailor shop was located on the farm and subsidized the income from farming. He also had a seamstress in the shop Miss Florell who had become his mistress. When he decided to immigrate, he sold the farm to Mister Treasure one of his right-hand man. Even though he had brought with him the money sold from the farm it was not enough to maintain the family long term, so he needed a job. At first, he decided to find a job within his trade and landed a job at Tip Top Tailors; however, tailoring in Canada was hard labour. Not only was he forced to stand over a hot iron all day, at the end of the day he was forced to battle the harshness of the Canadian winter. This was too hard on a man his age. He had to find something else. This he found as the night janitor for SKF a manufacturing plant in Scarborough. Noel again due to his punctuality, his Scottish heritage and strong networking skills was promoted to supervisor within 6 months. Noel's punctuality was another one of his strong skills, perhaps it was needed in a home with eight women and two men. It is amusing to note that at my sister's wedding his role was to take the bride to the church, my sister was running about 30 minutes behind schedule. Noel got so upset and insisted he was going to leave her Dolvis had to remind him that it was essential for the bride to be at the church as without the bride there could be no wedding!!!

Being a supervisor made the job more bearable as he could now train the younger men and do less physical work himself. Noel unlike Dolvis was not a fan of hard labour he was a great negotiator and networker and these skills were what he brought to the table. Four adults were now working full time however, salaries were small and the expense of food and shelter for ten still made for a tight budget. Dolvis started to recruit all age appropriate child into part time labour at Scarborough General Hospital. Lucky for us she was a dietician working in a hospital that required part time dietary help. Most of the part time workers were students and minimum age required was 15. Joy and Lelieth were the first recruits into that role the following year and hence additional financial aid towards food and utilities.

Canada at this time had not been introduced to the Brady Bunch and our family was a combined family. Dolvis had a daughter Joy prior to her marriage to Noel. Noel had six children with his first wife and one of his daughters was also named Joy. Dolvis decided to simplify and call Noel's daughter by her middle name Elizabeth and also to limit mentioning her daughter's last name which was Barrett. This was a conscious effort on her part to reduce questions and give the impression of one cohesive family.

Her administrative skills were also put to the test in managing such a large household budget. Dolvis sought jobs such as moonlighting as a cleaner to bring in extra funds. She would recruit other newly immigrated friends and family members to assist in these assignments. Chambers Foods Ltd. offered a plan she could not refuse where you would order frozen foods from their company and you would receive a freezer at a reduced monthly cost. This helped greatly in maintaining the food budget as well as the delivery of the foods were convenient at a time when busy working schedules left little time to shop for groceries, as well as poor transportation and one family car that was not always available for shopping needs.

Grocery shopping was an area that gave me one and one bonding time with my mom. My older siblings were responsible for cooking and housekeeping tasks in the home. I was also a picky eater with a preference for junk foods and sweets. Unfortunately, these treats were not essential on a tight budget but by accompanying my mom I was able to ensure that a box of cookies and ice cream were not left off the grocery list. Unaware to me at the time I was also learning great skills in budgeting and shopping.

Noel and Dolvis were fortunate to have excellent neighbours next door. Their new home was a semi-detached home where your neighbours could hear every noise coming from next door.

They were the typical nucleur Canadian family with one child a teenage son and a dog. They were quiet as a mouse but yet they enjoyed playing badminton with us over the fence and remained cordial and friendly to us the entire time we lived next door. This was not an easy task for a quiet lifestyle now forced to share their space with at least ten neighbors or more depending on which family member or friend my parents had recently helped gain entry into Canada. It was common practice for family or friends to request an invitation letter to come as a visitor and from there take their chances to apply for permanent residency.

My sister Lola had been left behind and not sponsored earlier as she had been working in Kingston and managing well on her own, however, in the summer of 1966 my eldest sister Norma tied the knot with her fiancee Clifford. Lola was the matron of honor and my dad was the only one that budget would allow to travel to the wedding. While on his visit he was not happy with the progress Lola was making in Jamaica and encouraged her to return to Canada with him to seek her fortune elsewhere. Lola had been working in the healthcare field as a health care aide or what we now call a personal support worker. So, it was in the summer of 1966 one more family member was added to our already large abode. Lola who was already an adult at 22 was thus forced to try and sponsor herself as she could no longer be sponsored as a dependent child. Ivy Ellison also came over from England that summer with her own personal reasons of wanting to seek her fortune elsewhere.

Ivy was the cousin who had received me as a child in Kingston but later went to England after she was sponsored by her brother Winston. Dolvis was also her godmother so when she decided to try her luck in Canada she sent a letter to my mom asking for an invitation letter, however; Dolvis advised her that her quota was full based on her large family arriving earlier in the year. Lucky for Ivy she was able to travel without that letter as she was now a British citizen, however; Dolvis did accommodate her in her home until she got settled. Caribbean families were trying to make a go of their new life in the 1960s and helping other family members was the norm.

Canada was suddenly seen as a new frontier and everyone wanted to try their luck in Canada

*Picture of our first home in Canada on Allanford Road in Agincourt.
Lola my sister is posing on front porch steps on a Sunday as was our usual
custom to take pics on a nice Sunday after the family meal!*

CHAPTER 4

||||||||||||||||||||||||||||||||||||||||||||||||||||||||||||||||||||

LIVING THE DREAM!!

Life started to evolve slowly with hard work and persistance for Dolvis and Noel with the help of everyone pitching in. Noel was then able to put together the money from land sold in Jamaica and help of all to buy the home we were renting. We now owned our first home in Canada. The basement was then renovated and 2 more bedrooms and a washrocm with a shower to allow for accommodating the ever-increasing family. There was now 7 bedrooms and 2.5 bathrooms in our home. Dolvis continued to work extra hours at the hospital and take on part time cleaning as needed to supplement household income.

Noel was not a man driven to do hard work. Even though he was a farmer in Jamaica his role was managing the inherited family farm and he always had workers who worked the farm. He did, however, have natural skills in real estate investing and would take time out to look at homes that he could possibly buy for rental income. The next two years my parents continued to assist cousins, distant relatives, and friends to immigrate and the extra beds in our home were always full.

The family size now dictated the need for transportation by car; the winters in those early years were extreme with lots of snow and everyone was taking the bus and feeling the extreme of the winter cold. On Sundays there was an elder Mr. Burridge from the church with a station wagon that made it his duty to pick up the Lambie family. Mr. Burridge is etched in my memory as he also had a dry-cleaning business which we supported. He would drop off and pick up our laundry on Sundays as well as drive us to church. As a hardworking self-employed businessman, he was always tired, and it was his usual practice to get his best sleep during the church services. Every Sunday like clockwork as children we would look over to see how soon and how long Mr. Burridge would sleep thoughout the services.

Sundays in own home was always a family celebration and a day of Thanksgiving. My older siblings would help with the preparation of Sunday dinner which was a feast. There was usually baked chicken, rice and peas, cabbage, and carrot, jello salad, ice cream and pie for dessert. As already mentioned, we were not a quiet family. Sunday dinner was always debate time at the dinner table with my brother usually in the role of moderator insisting us ladies lower our voices when arguments got too heated. Noel, however. was our closure who would promptly state I need to digest and enjoy my food so shut up until I'm done eating. That would have us scampering off and start cleaning up to be continued the following week.

Keith, my brother was the first to buy a car it was a white Chevrolet and he was so good at dropping my sisters and picking them up. My older siblings were getting used to the social scene in Canada and with his help would go to the movies and the new West Indian night spots. My dad was getting very uncomfortable with the free social rules of dating in Canada especially as it relates to young women. Noel was a very traditional man with traditional values; what men could do women could not do etc. Surprisingly, he had very modern ideas and thoughts on education. He felt strongly that education was important and vital for not only men but also women. So much so that he felt as women it was important to put off dating or any impediment which was men and their needs until you had achieved a university degree. This would ensure that you were an independent woman not needing a man to supply your needs. Noel had eight legal daughters and perhaps his modern thoughts also stemmed from the fact that he did not want to be saddled with the expense of having to take care of any of his daughters. As a result, my mom was forced to intervene at every interval on our behalf but unfortunately due to her work schedule she could not be there at every call. This resulted in a major scene between my father and my younger half-sister Lelieth when she decided to accept the invitation for a date with a family friend.

Tanny was the son of my mother's cousin Mrs. Baxter with whom my mother had first stayed when she arrived in Canada. We were quite close to this family and their background was well documented and known. They had spent numerous occasions at our home and that is how a friendship had developed between the two young people. Never-the-less when my sister requested his permission to go on a date with this young man my father refused. Lelieth was now 16 and of age according to the rules and norms of our new country to date socially. My sister insisted she was going and got dressed to leave for her date. Upon arrival of her date my father was not having it he slapped my sister, barred the door and told the young man to leave and that he was no longer welcome in our home. The battle of the culture norms was now active and on fire in our home. My sister bore the embarrassment and anger of my father but for the rest of us she had broken him down and paved the way for an easier transition to our later years of social dating. I know I am getting ahead of myself but Lelieth did go on to become successful lawyer with a practice in Jamaica. Perhaps this very battle with her father shaped her to become a fighter and legal representative in later life. Our parents were indeed our role models whose prime purpose was to teach, shape and mold us into better and productive human beings.

By 1969 it was obvious we needed another family home with more room, so my father bought a second larger home just a little bit further north at Victoria Park and Finch in a new subdivision. With his strong investment skills, he kept our first home as rental property for my elder siblings. Norma and her husband had also immigrated and needed a place to stay. Life in Jamaica had changed for the new couple. They were both professionals, Norma was a pharmacist and Clifford an engineer but still they were not having an easy transition into middle class living and hence wanted to try their hands at the new opportunities in Canada.

Jamaica in the late 60s was a newly independent nation still going through a lot of growing pains brought about from the shift from colonial rule to that of an economy supporting the common good of the rising middle class of black heritage. This middle class was now taking use of the new educational opportunities open to them but at the end of the day still needed entry into high end positions that were dominated by those of Syrian and Asian heritage.

The retail businesses were primarily owned by the Chinese immigrants who immigrated to Jamaican to set up their own family businesses with the intention of passing that business on to their immediate family. Their practice was as well to send back to China for a wife or husband for their children to carry on their family legacy. The middle class majority of black ethnic background were forced to use or utilize higher education as a means of getting themselves out of marginal poverty but still found it difficult to compete for a high level job. The practice was for these positions to stay within the elitist families. Canada was just starting to open up as a major player in the economic market and doors were now open to immigration from the Caribbean. Canada needed professional workers, trade workers and unskilled workers. My sister and her husband felt that the opportunities were elsewhere as they were both young and educated and willing to learn and work in Canada and hopefully return to Jamaica with more honed skills. My brother Keith and sister Lola were also staying in that home as well and made it possible for shared rental space while they adjusted to their new life in Canada.

The appeal of Canada was now attractive to Norma and Clifford and with the help of Dolvis and Noel and an affordable place to rent they made their move. Upon arriving they became renters in the home along with Keith and 3 other siblings who were all now over 18. This now allowed Noel and Dolvis to move into their second home closer to the Canadian ideal of a nuclear family with just five younger siblings myself included. They had successful accomplished the first part of their job as parents and purpose in getting the older children settled, and on their way to making a better life in Canada.

Norma and Clifford came to Canada already educated in their respective professions. They however had a rude awakening as Norma needed more schooling in order to practice as a pharmacist in Canada, so she sought work elsewhere. Lucky for her she was very personable and found work at Bell Canada as one of their phone representatives. Clifford also found work in a small engineering firm and both were on their way to make life in Canada. Lola had a respectable job at Providence Villa as a health care aide; Joy was working as an administrative clerk at Toronto General Hospital and Keith had landed a job at Honeywell after first working as a porter at Scarborough General Hospital. Dorothy who had travelled with Noel and was in her late teens was able to return to high school and then go on to university. Noel and Dolvis dream of higher education was finally starting to become a reality for the younger siblings.

In the winter of 1971, we settled into their new home with five siblings still in school. Lelieth, Elizabeth, Charmaine, and I were now in high school and Sharon was in junior high school. We were happy to be in a new home in a new subdivision. Everything was new and clean and all around us they were still building new homes. It was winter and there was mud and snow all around from the left-over cement and unfinished construction. We were now also a two-car family. Dolvis busy schedule and the lack of public transportation in our new home had made it necessary for her to get a car of her own. Dolvis had never driven in Jamaica but nothing was impossible for her so it was with great pride she took the plunge of taking driving lessons, studying the manual so that on her first attempt she was able to pass the driving test and achieved yet another milestone to independence in her new country.

Dolvis was a petite woman of about five feet two but she loved everything big, so it was no surprise that her first car had to be big. Her choice was the Ford Torino in lime green which was a popular colour that year. That way she could not be missed on the road and as a new driver it gave her comfort in knowing that she was protected by the big steel body of that car. Dolvis had become active in her church and had taken on singing in the choir as well as helping with events at the church. The new home was further away from her home church as well as her work so having a car made it so much easier and gave her the freedom to come and go as was needed. Noel had gotten a car the year after he arrived but he was not comfortable driving in snow or rain so it always had created a problem when she needed to get somewhere and he was hesitant about driving in bad weather. Noel also was working nights and had a different sleep schedule than herself. He needed to sleep in the daytime. His practice was to sleep for about 6 hours in the daytime. Then he would get up for supper and go back to sleep for 2 hours before leaving for his night shift. Her work schedule was 7am to 3pm and that left her time to go to choir practice in the evenings and moonlight doing cleaning jobs. For the rest of the family the lack of transportation meant we had a twenty- minute walk after the bus dropped us off at the last stop just north of Sheppard. I can remember seeing grass-snakes on the ground while we walked home along mostly farm-lands with greenery and small ponds. This was our nature walk and means of exercise prior to the invention of gyms and gym membership.

Dolvis had now also started a part time business baking Jamaican rum cakes. This was a skill she had perfected while in Jamaica. Now with a lot of immigration from the islands there was a need for cakes for the holidays and most importantly the wedding cakes. The Caribbean culture tradition was to have tiered rum cakes decorated for weddings. It required fruits to be soaked or boiled in rum and wine for months ahead to give the cakes a strong flavour of alcohol blended with the dried fruits and spices. Brides to be paid handsomely for this cake at their weddings and additional side cakes would be ordered. The tradition dictated that additional cakes were cut up and each guest was given a sample of the cake to take home as a gift.

These cakes freeze very well due to the alcohol content and once they were thawed, they could be refreshed with wine to bring back their freshness. One of the tiers would be kept for your first anniversary and another tier for the birth of your first child. Dolvis knew she would also make more money if she was able to decorate the cakes as well, so she promptly signed up for decorating classes in royal icing.

Royal icing was a popular method of using sugar and butter as a base to create a fluffy but sweet cream for decorating the cakes and creating shapes such as flowers to add artistic design to the cakes. Dolvis delighted in not only the baking of the cake but she found the artistic designing of the décor of the wedding cakes to be relaxing and enjoyable. My fondest memories are watching her staying up late into the night after receiving an order for her cakes. She would take time to prepare the mixture and cakes would need to be cooled after baking so that the décor could be done two or three days later. Marzipan which is an almond paste would be used to cover the rum cake prior to applying the icing as it would give a smooth finish similar to putting foundation on the face before applying makeup. The icing once mixed to the right texture would then be squeezed though a piping bag and with careful hands applied to the cake to create first a smooth finish and then a variety of designs including intricate rose petals. This truly was a work of art and her artistic expression to the world!!

Noel had found his own groove in his pursuit for real estate investing and our first home was now a rental for the extension of our family. Noel would then take time on Sundays to walk through our new neighbourhood. New homes were in the process of being built daily as the area was now expanding into new suburban homes. This he found exciting as he believed that land was man's greatest source of wealth and necessary for survival. He was constantly on the lookout for opportunities to invest. His job at SKF was simply a means to pay his bills and secure some retirement fund as his goal was to return to Jamaica as soon as his children were self-sufficient so that he could relax and get out of the harsh winter weather.

Lola and Joy were now considering moving to the United States to make some quick money to return to Canada for investment and Norma and Clifford wanted to set out in an apartment on their own. Keith now had a steady girlfriend and was saving to get his own home. The time was right for him to now sell that home and acquire more rental properties.

Our family was now coming into a groove at our new home at Corinthian Boulevard in Scarborough. At first the daunting prospect of moving to a community with very few homes was very dismal to everyone. Dirt and mud lay all around us and a constant number of construction workers mostly from Italy all around. As women we were constantly heckled while walking past them as was their custom in their native country. Our new community was a mix match of many ethnic groups. Our next door neighbours were from Germany and across from us was an Italian family and to the right of us a South Asian family from Trinidad.

Our parents were slowly settling into their new surroundings and adjusting to work and home schedules. Both Dolvis and Noel drove and owed a car, and this was now a necessity as buses only went to Sheppard Avenue and we lived closer to Finch. It would have been a treacherous walk for them but as young people we had the physical capability to endure that walk when necessary. All of us were now working part time at Scarboro General Hospital, with the exception of Sharon who was still too young to work. Coming home at night presented many challenges in the winter with snowy and dark conditions. Most of the time we just made it home just in time before we could turn into icicles. It was a twenty to thirty minute walk up a deserted unpaved dirt road with snow coming half way up ones knees and the wind blowing you back with every step. It was so dark you could barely see the outline of the trees that lined your path along the way. We usually came home in pairs as none of us felt safe enough to walk that winter path home on our own. Tears would start to come to your eyes from the chilling cold but by then you could barely feel your face. Your hands were now so numb you dared not try to bring to your face and take them from your coat pockets where they were needed for extra warmth. Even with two of us walking we were always keeping watch and saying a silent prayer that we would reach home safely. We also knew not to call my dad Noel to give us a ride on those snowy cold days. Noel was a Caribbean Man who was not comfortable driving on snow and hated the bitter cold. His regular ritual when coming in from the cold was to apply white rum which had been soaked with pimento to his face and neck to ward off any danger of a flu or pneumonia.

Yes, those early winters of the 60's and 70's were harsh but necessary to teach us determination and perseverance!!!

As young people we were naturally bored and needed new friends and to find our own sense of community. Corinthian Boulevard in time proved to be just that for us.

Noel and Dolvis had been encouraged to move there by another family friend that they had formed alliance with the Mulgraves. Mr Mulgrave was a short, quiet man who had immigrated to Canada in the 1950's and had worked on the railroad. He was used to the harsh winters in Canada and had sponsored his sweetheart Anne from Jamaica. Anne was a slim woman slightly taller than her husband. They had two daughters who had immigrated with her from Jamaica and four more children born in Canada and a fifth child they had adopted from Jamaica who had lost her mother at an early age. Mr. Mulgrave was a dedicated family man who worked hard to support his large family. They also had a strong religious background and attended a very traditional Penticostal church that had striict rules. Their home had no television and the girls had to wear their skirts at a modest length just below their knee.

Anne Mulgrave was a health care aide but also a hard worker and industrious woman. She also boarded young children in her home. This was a practice as many newcomers from the

Caribbean were single women with children. They worked as nannies living in homes full time and needed someone to take care of their preschool children. Daycare and subsidized day care was not yet available and these mothers needed after hours and weekend care for their children. The children would live full time with the Mulgrave's and be picked up to spend time with their mothers on their day off. This required teamwork and the Mulgrave children would assist Anne in her second occupation of in-home care.

The Mulgrave family was a special family as they also had a special need son named Lorne. This was the first time our family had seen or was exposed to a special need child. Lorne was a warm loving child and was allowed to freely go about from our home to their home especially since for the first year there was no fence so everyone just walked across the grass to visit and spend time.

The Mulgraves' was our first bond of another black family in Canada. Three of their girls were the same age as myself and my younger sister and we were now starting to feel comfortable in our new home with friends that looked like us and had similar experiences.

Since our parents were busy earning a living, we had a lot of free time to make friends. We then made it our duty to observe black families moving into the new homes and would then make it our business to knock on the door and introduce ourselves. This resulted in a strong community of black families and mentors in our community. Through this process we were introduced to the diverse families from the Caribbean who moved and became a part of our community.

These included our cousin the Muirs' Carmen and her husband Hasbin. Carmen was a hairstylist and her husband a taxi-driver. The Muirs were a childless couple. Hasbin was a tall handsome man and Carmen a petite woman who loved to dress and carry herself with style and grace. The Anderson's from Guyana moved in the same year as well. Percy Anderson was a professor at York University and his wife Bea a teacher at a local high school. They had two daughters close in age to my younger sister and have been best friends since we knocked at their door that first day. They were also a couple of huge contrast Percy was a small built man who enjoyed cooking and baking for his family. Bea was tall for a woman but had an elegant-reserved air.

The Deans were a large family from St Vincent with a strong single mom at the helm. Mrs. Dean was a non-nonsense woman with strict rules for her twin sons and young daughter. They were also fast friends and boyfriends as we were very happy to finally have some attractive young black men living in our community.

Finally, the Thomblisons a family of Caribbean descent but who had first immigrated to England and had now made Canada their home.

Mr. Thomblinson had immigrated due to his skill as an electrician. Canada had sent out a call for tradesmen and with four small children their family saw it as an opportunity for their young family. They were a beautiful couple especially Mrs. Thomblison who after four children still had a flawless cocoa complexion and could still turn men's head due to both her striking facial beauty and hourglass figure. Their small children were a hand full but provided babysitting income for myself and my younger sister Sharon.

Dolvis was quite content with her family expanding and exploring new options, however she still had her domestic struggles with Noel. Noel suffered from the disease of infidelity which was a common affliction among men of that era. Noel was still in communication with his mistress in Jamaica and had sent her an invitation letter to come to Canada. So it was that sometime in the early 70's Ms. Florrell arrived in Canada with the help of Noel.

Ms. Florell was a simple woman with a daughter from a previous relationship. She was trained as a seamstress. Noel and his mistress had gotten together because of her skills when he needed a seamstress to assist him in his tailoring business in St Mary. Mrs Florell needed a lot of financial support as a single woman coming to Canada with no working skills and this Noel provided. Both herself and her daughter were settled in an apartment in Canada. Dolvis never discussed our father's relationship with this woman but it was well observed on Sundays that it was his day to visit her home.

Dolvis would leave for church on Sundays and my father would leave our home and return on Sunday afternoon in time for Sunday dinner. This was the routine for most of the remaining years they were in Canada. Noel had a rule or code that explained and rationalized his behavior. First and four most he was from the old boys' school that believed what a man could do a woman could not. He also felt that he showed respect for his home and his marriage by always coming home at a respectable time and never sleeping out at night. This he demonstrated when in later years he was giving advice to my sister's adulterous husband and he chastised him for his lack of respect in bringing the woman into the family home and sleeping out at nights. Noel however, failed to advise him that the behavior and the very act of adultery was wrong.

Dolvis still had a strong commitment to her marriage and even more a strong faith and conviction in God. She decided to stay in her marriage and continue to pray for the salvation of her husband's soul. Dolvis decided however, to impart on a financial venture of her own and also to keep her finances separate from her husband. After all she had three legal children with Noel and an older daughter Joy who was solely her child to protect. Dolvis decided it was time to own her own home. After two years living in a new home owed by Noel, she took steps to acquire her own home with the help of the favourite and popular Caribbean realtor at that time Olga Rigg.

CHAPTER 5

||||||||||||||||||||||||||||||||||||||||||||||||||||||||||||

THE CIRCLE OF WOMEN!!

OLGA RIGGS

Dolvis in her struggles for survival in her relationship with Noel would not have survived if not for some great relationships with some strong women who were her friends and business partners.

Olga Rigg was one of those ladies. Olga was a survivor from St. Catherines Jamaica who had made her way out of that island after an early marriage, divorce and five children, to seek her fortune in Canada. Olga had travelled as a nanny to Alberta in the early years. After settling there as most of the immigrant nannies at that time she found her way to Toronto. She then proceeded to sponsor her second husband and slowly sponsor her children in Jamaica to join her. All accomplished after having two other children in Canada with her second husband Rudolph Rigg affectionately called Ruddy.

Olga had a very vibrant and outgoing personality which equipped her well in her choice to return to school and get a realtor license. As a result, in those early years she was the market consultant to most of the recent immigrant men and women in the area whose main goal in those years was to own their own home. Olga was a woman of voluptuous built with a wicked sense of humour and a mischievous laugh that radiated as she moved through a room. She also had a youthful exuberance and a zest for life that was contagious. Dolvis on the other hand was very reserved with a quiet demeanor and elegance. The contrast of the two women was striking and obvious to everyone who saw them together.

So it was that when my mother decided it was time to own her home Olga assisted her in that dream. With Olga's help this home was truly the best home we had owned to date. It was a backsplit home on a corner lot. This meant the home was primarily a bungalow with different levels and no basement as all levels were above ground. It was a beautiful all brick home with dark brown coloured bricks. There were three ample bedrooms on the upper level with a shared full bathroom, kitchen dining and living area all in wood parkway very popular at that time. On the lower level was a family room and bathroom with a large tile shower and room to add on two more bedrooms. The majority of the neighbourhood at that time were Europeans of Italian descent and their homes were famous for their great gardens, beautiful stone and tile work inside and outside of their homes. Dolvis was not one that cared much for gardening so it would be a challenge for her to keep up to her neighbours' gardens but she did like order and a sense of community so she couldn't help but fall in love with the home.

Dolvis had been introduced to Olga by Carmen Muir who had also bought her home from Olga.

Olga and the Rigg family would later become a lot closer to the Lambie family as I later started to date and fell in love with her son Larry and had my only child a son with him while still a teenager in high school.

Dolvis was not happy with my relationship with Larry who ran with a fast crowd. It was years later I realized why my attraction for Larry was so strong and where my parents had failed in parenting their immigrant children.

They had immigrated with a goal in mind for their family for better education and upward mobility and without realizing it had turned their back on their cultural heritage. Dolvis had completely immersed herself into religion at the expense of music or any of the cultural arts. Noel as well failed to bring any cultural identity to the family and his main interest and priority was education or how he viewed education by the broader society.

Caribbean music or the arts was not encouraged or demonstrated in my home. I was a very bright student who learned easily but with adolescent came a desire to understand who I was and where I came from. We also lived in the suburbs where there was little black or Caribbean influence or identification.

It was against all this backdrop that the Riggs proved to be a welcome and needed form of education in my life at the time. Their home was filled with music of all types and not just popular music but black music from the Caribbean and the USA. Larry was an amateur DJ who collected current black music from all over and prided himself in being the first to have any new music. The family including Olga loved to dance and would just play music and then practice all the latest dances while introducing nuances of their own. Everyone would join in the lyrics of the song as most of the family not only danced well but could carry a tune. They were natural entertainers and dancers. They had a cousin by the name of Carlton who recently died who was a natural storyteller. The family would gather in their living area, and he would delight in telling a story with his usual twist and sarcastic slant and everyone would laugh. Music and dancing would always follow with everyone taking a turn at their own interpretation of music through their own volley of steps and movement.

Larry's style of dancing was very sensual and erotic and though shocking at first it forced me to express my own sexual and artistic freedom that was so highly blocked in the reserved holiness of my own family. The family would have parties and attend parties whereever Larry was playing the music. Myself and my sibling were therefore introduced to strong cultural arts and freedom of expression of the Caribbean. It was through this exchange that we learned to dance and develop an education and introduction to many of the musical artists from the Caribbean and North America.

My dad had not envisioned that when he prayed for his children to become educated that education would need to take different forms and instructions.

Dolvis and Olga because of their vastly different family values maintained primarily a business relationship. Even after I had given birth to their grand-child their relationship remained cordial and business-like. Dolvis did also buy a second property for investment from Olga, a condo for Joy my elder sister and her eldest daughter.

Joy and Lola had crossed the border to the States to make some quick cash and Joy had been saving and amassed enough funds for a down payment. Dolvis wanted to ensure that her daughter had a home of her own to invest in and live when she decided to return to Canada. Olga and Dolvis went to view the new condos being built in the Don Mills area and with Joy's approval the condo was bought. Dolvis continued to manage it for Joy until her return to Canada. It was rented it to a cousin, Faye and her family who had recently migrated to Canada. Dolvis then managed the payments and started Joy on her investment journey.

ANNIE MULGRAVE

Annie Mulgrave now deceased was another close friend of Dolvis. Anne was an attractive dark-skinned slim no-non-sense woman. She was very observant and would look you up and down when you first meet as if to decide if you were fit to be in her presence. It was Anne and her husband that had encouraged Noel to buy their second home at Corinthian Boulevard as they were already owners in the subdivision. Annie was a natural entrepreneur who worked as a nurse's aide at the hospital but also ran a boarding home for children in her home. Annie and Dolvis shared the love of the Lord even though Annie's church was far more conservative than hers'.

Dolvis home had a television set and my mom did not dictate how we chose to dress. Miniskirts were in and as young ladies we were very much into the fashion of the day. Mom also did not mind the fact that we loved going to parties or the movies or even dating. All of these activities were banned in the Mulgraves' home as their church dismissed all worldy passions and possesions as sin.

Nevertheless, the two women bonded and would share their experiences. This was a great asset to Dolvis when she ventured into owning her own home as she did not receive the financial support from Noel and had to seek alternate sources of income to maintain her home.

Dolvis was currently employed full time at Scarborough General Hospital as a dietician but she had to maintain a home, a car and a family which was now reduced to her three natural children with her husband Noel. Noel was subsidizing his mistress and only providing funds for food and some utilities. Dolvis had bought the home and it was her responsibility to cover mortgage and all other major bills. Dolvis was determined and embarked on two different business ventures. The first was foster care of children. No doubt here she was encouraged and sought counsel from Annie. Annie was boarding children of West Indian parents but Dolvis decided to go another route by taking in foster children.

Dolvis had a background in nursing and after some thought and the influence of Anne she decided she would foster special needs children. My mom now had only her three natural children at home including me We were all teenagers going through the pains of adolescent, not exactly the best time to introduce a new in-home business. My mom felt strongly that the children with physical and mental disabilities would pose challenges in feeding and caring but would also provide opportunities for love and support.

The ground level basement was converted into three bedrooms to provide bedrooms for these children. While she waited on approval and placement for the children Dolvis also took in a divorced man with his son who had newly immigrated to Canada and needed a temporary place to stay until he got a full-time job and became settled. They were a quiet family and the son Trevor became lifelong friends with our family for many years to come.

The introduction of the special-needs children brought a whole new dynamics to our family life. As much as this was a thought our plan for extra income; these children brought so much unconditional love and unforeseen blessings into our home. They also provided a means for Dolvis to give and receive love especially in areas where she had not felt loved.

There was Mary who was mentally challenged and so full of love and a caring spirit. Tony who was physically challenged and had difficulty walking and Eddie who loved to eat and would eat everything in sight, so keys had to be put on all food storage units including the freezer. Vicky suffered from brain damage and could neither talk nor walk but was always smiling. My mom had a soft spot for her as she was the hardest to get care relief for as she had to be changed and lifted in and out of her wheelchair but would always smile. Our very first child Jane instantly became like family. Jane was about six years old with Down Syndrome. She was very fair with blond hair and had a bright smile that just warmed up the room. Jane's parents were university professors who had a late life pregnancy and were too busy with their career to keep her at home. They would, however, visit her on weekends and take her home for visits. Jane was always happy and loved to eat all foods including our Jamaican dishes. She was a delightful addition to our home and stayed with us until she was able to go on her own.

Dolvis would work full time at the hospital and then be home in time to accept her new charges from school, give them supper and get them ready for bed. There was now joy and a purpose in having them depend on her and she was loving her second job. Still with a mortgage and property taxes to pay and no major help from a spouse Dolvis turned another part time hobby into a business. That was the business of baking Jamaican rum cakes. In this side business she partnered with another family friend Carmen Lambie-Muir.

CARMEN LAMBIE-MUIR

Carmen Lambie-Muir was the niece of Noel. She was a born entrepreneur. She had left Jamaica via the nanny program and arrived at first via Western Canada. As much of those ladies did back then as soon as possible they found themselves to Toronto to live the dream. Carmen also had left her boyfriend behind and went back and married Hasbin and sponsored him to join her in Canada. With no known skills she decided that hairdressing was her calling and was one of the 1st black woman to enter the hairstyling school in Toronto.

Hairstyling was the business needed for black women in the 60's. Black women wanted to have a more acceptable look and were having challenges dealing with the kinks in their hair. Hot combing was the process to straighten the hair by taking a hot comb and pulling through the hair until it became straight. It required some skill and steady hands as most women did at one time or another receive burns to the scalps and forehead from not being careful. This process also reversed back if the hair got wet or sweaty, so it was important to repeat the process every time the hair was washed or at least every two weeks.

Carmen was on to something as it was a necessity and growing business with the growing pool of Caribbean women now immigrating to Canada.

Carmen set up shop at Bathurst and Bloor which at the time in the late 60's and 70's was the business centre of the recent Afro Caribbean immigrants. She now became without really trying the network queen of the women at that time. All the women came to her shop to get their hair straightened and all the latest news and views were shared. Carmen and Dolvis were cousin in law hence news of her cake business was spread through the community and every bride to be would place an order for the wedding cake. The wedding cake was the ultimate order usually a 3-tier cake and at least two side cakes. Dolvis business was off with the aid of her entrepreneurial cousin. But they did not stop there. Carmen loved to cook and was good at the Caribbean curry goat, rice and peas and beef soup. Carmen beauty shop was open Tuesdays to Saturdays and her off day was always Sundays and Mondays. Hence it gave her amply time to start her catering business. Carmen would cook and hire servers for the wedding party and Dolvis would provide the cakes. Carmen had access to photographers, DJs and dressmakers who could design and sew dresses for the bride.

The stage was set!!

Carmen Saturdays were full indeed, after standing all day at the beauty parlour she would be off to catering and her Saturday would end sometime Sunday morning. For most that would be enough, but Carmen also had another side in home business on Sundays. It was soup and tea leaf reading at Carmen's home. Carmen had a business partnership with a Portuguese fortune teller Maria who would come to her home on Sundays to read tea leaves. We were never sure of Carmen's percentage cut in this business as she would provide tea and Caribbean soup for all attendees. Maria's usual reading always saw an engagement ring in the future of all the eligible single ladies. This Carmen encouraged as she was also an amateur matchmaker and had successfully arranged a few marriages in her time.

Dolvis and Carmen connected because of their strong love of family, home, and quest for opportunities to make extra money. Dolvis was not a fan of the fortune teller as she was a church goer and did not believe that God sanctioned the works of any fortune teller but that was an area that she did not take part in. She would always pray for Carmen's soul that she would one day become a Christian and attend church with her on Sundays. That was never to be as both ladies died still firm in their beliefs and purpose for living. Dolvis as a nurse had a scientific mind and insured that we also believed in the medical profession. Carmen was a great believer in the healing power of the herbs and medicinal oils from the Caribbean. So much so that even though she suffered from high blood pressure she seldom took any of the medications given to her by the doctors. She would drink Cerasee a bush grown in Jamaica which is known as a remedy for lowering blood pressure and continue to eat her salt fish and add salt to her diet. Carmen was the holistic healer of the family and that gifting was surely missed on her passing as well.

If Dolvis had a best friend at this junction in her life I would say it was Carmen. Even though their spiritual ideology was vastly different there was mutual trust and respect between the two ladies. They also shared each other secrets and ran partners together and would assist each other in times of financial need such as when buying a home.

Here is pic of my sister Lelieth's wedding. Cake was baked and decorated by Dolvis as her gift to her stepdaughter. Carmen was the caterer of the food. Both Lelieth and her husband Patrick were the wedding planner and designer of wedding party with theme of African style which gained popularity in the early 70's with the black power movement.

Here are dishes set up for the catered wedding party ready to be served to the guests. Carmen would hire and pay helpers to serve food and clean up but the cooking was primarily her task.

Partners were a great investment tool for these women. It created forced saving and a bulk sum of money to assist with large purchases or vacation plans.

A weekly sum of money was given to a banker in the group for a predetermined time. Each week the banker would give all the money to one person in the group. This would continue until everyone in the group had received a weekly sum of total funds given. There was no interest given but it created a forced saving and group members could choose which week to take their draw or funds based on need. For example if you needed $1000 to buy an item within a week you could request an early draw to get funds quickly knowing full well you will have to put back those funds for others to get their funds later. It required trust and faith that all parties would pay up and allow all to benefit in the long run. Most of these investment pools did very well as new immigrants did not have credit available from the bank so they had to look to alternate means to build and receive necessary funds.

Both Dolvis and Carmen had pooled together several times in the partner agreement to get a deposit for their home, and also to buy furniture and travel.

Dolvis as one of the first within her family to come to Canada provided mentorship for all women family members. One of her main source of mentorship to family members were through job referral. Dolvis was instrumental in referring jobs to her goddaughter Ivy when she arrived in Canada. Ivy was hired as food supervisor at Scarboro General Hospital where they both worked together as part of the kitchen staff. Joyce or Ethel May a cousin as we later discovered was her legal name was referred by Dolvis into Scarborough General Housekeeping section where she worked until she retired.

Dolvis was also instrumental in keeping Joyce's son Calvin out of the Children's Aid system by volunteering her home for his care when he arrived in Canada and would not adhere to the rules in his new home with his mother and stepfather. This was a problem for many mothers at the time. The usual pattern for Caribbean families was to get settled and then later send for their children. In most cases these children were left with their grandparents who were soft on disciple. This would sometimes result in hostility and lack of bonding with parents and hence rebellion on the part of the pre-teen child once they arrived in Canada.

So, it was in the case of Calvin that Dolvis stepped in to allow him to continue to live within the family and not be taken over by the Children's Aid Society.

Today CAS society has created a kinship program, but this was something that Caribbean immigrants did naturally. A family member was always happy to step in as parent to assist with a child so that the mother could further studies and get settled.

Having Calvin in our home also created a turbulent and explosive dynamic at times. Our home had always been a female-centred home and learning to adjust our home to an adolescent boy in house took major compromises. Dolvis was very hospitable and was impartial with her treatment of Calvin so much so that they formed a special bond. He was encouraged to be involved in sports and took up track. He also had a voracious appetite and did not obey rules of curfew or chores so there were constant battles with us girls and our new male resident on those violations.

Calvin was a strong willed and determined young man and Dolvis encouraged and supported his free and independent thinking. So much so that he later went on to create, start and run a successful moving company for over 30 years.

Dolvis and her circle of women without knowing it was setting the groundwork and building each other through their entrepreneurial skills and encouragement to own homes and build businesses. Education was also a tool as most of the women had undergone training to get certified in some occupation or trade. This initial process gained them access to a skill which provided stability to the family. This then allowed them the freedom to venture out into other areas of business or creative interest to make extra funds, broaden their horizon and create a passion and purpose to their daily living.

Mentorship then came naturally to the young people in their family and the community. Families were striving, growing, and learning with the cumulative experiences and opportunities and these women pioneers were continually blazing the trail by setting new goals and moving on to new targets.

Dolvis continued to do what she did best by taking on new challenges. A friend referred her to another single mother who was working full time and fast tracking in her career, she had no time to take care of her daughter Audrey, she was given Dolvis's number to call for fostering.

Dolvis didn't bat an eye and welcomed Audrey into her home where she attended school and studied while her mother continued to build on her career and maintain the family home she had bought in the suburbs of Scarborough. This was similar to what Dolvis had observed her friend Anne Mulgrave do in the early years with the toddlers. Audrey proved to be a very bright young lady who just needed care and attention. She continued to thrive under the new arrangement with daily access to her mother Verona via telephone calls and visits on her mother's days off. Our last contact with Audrey we were happy to hear that she had graduated and went on to university with intentions of going to law school.

Dolvis was content that she had taken the plunge of home ownership by faith not knowing exactly where the funds were coming from to support mortgage payments and all the other responsibilities that come along with home ownership. It had taken her places and had her use talents she never knew she had but she had endured.

Pic of Dolvis's home that she acquired on her own. It was a corner lot back split. In front is Lola who loved taking pictures with her son Yerodin just months old.

CHAPTER 6

||||||||||||||||||||||||||||||||||||||||||||||||||||||

LIVING THE LIFE!!

Dolvis and Noel had weathered the storm, and both were now enjoying life on their own terms. Still together as a married couple but with their own rules of co-existence.

Dolvis did have one final passion and that was to have a separate home devoted to special needs children. Unfortunately, with Noel not on board Dolvis had to abort that goal. She had managed to buy a separate home for that purpose and was in the process of setting that home up to accommodate the children, but Noel was hell bent on returning back to Jamaica to retire.

He had set a goal of returning after all his children had finished university or college and were gainfully employed. Noel had never fully adapted to the Canadian way of life. He had been forced to take on work as a janitor at night which was a blow to his ego and his need for respect and notoriety. In Jamaica as the owner and manager of a farm he was respected and known by everyone in the community of Wood Park. He also sat on the agricultural board and was well thought of in the agricultural circles. Unfortunately, that kind of respect did not come to him when he immigrated to Canada. He longed for the days when he could lounge on his veranda look up at the blue skies, hear the dogs barking and just feel the warmth of the sun and the cooling breeze from the sea. Not to mention having neighbours pass by and greet him fondly with the warmth and down-home friendly nature that is common in the islands.

He longed to hear the Good Morning Mr. Lambie in that broken patois and the small talk about weather and politics of the day. He felt he was due and longed for that type of recognition respect and acknowledgment again. He no longer wanted to work hard for a living. He could also get back to waking up early when the cock crows and getting settled into bed when nature intended naturally at sunset which was about 7pm; and not this business of clocks turned back and forth to prolong the day and bring confusion to his mind body and soul. Jamaica time was his time and he had endured the punishment for the sake of his children but enough was enough. His time was now while he was still young enough to enjoy the sunshine, the beach, plant a few crops and just have some lazy hazy days. Jamaica was calling and he was ready!!!

Life was good they had endured some challenging years when his first daughter Charmaine had rebelled and move out from their home due to the cultural clashes and agreements on curfews and dating. Children in Canada had a new independence and entitlement that he had never experienced with his older children. His older girls were not allowed to date, and they would never have considered disobeying him. From the onset of entry into Canada he had to battle Lelieth and after that things got worse for the younger girls.

Charmaine was very stubborn and loved to party and would not adhere to any curfew. Finally, she left the home only to be pregnant the next year. Noel was beside himself. Charmaine had been one of his favourite daughter as she was outgoing and very social just like him. Everyone liked her as she was always smiling and pleasant to be around. This was not why he had made all those sacrifices in selling the farm and coming to Canada. He had a major argument with Dolvis and blamed her for being too lenient on the girls by allowing them to date at 16 because that was the custom in Canada. He did not care what they did in Canada and now this was the result of it all. None of the older girls had gotten pregnant because he had kept a tight rein on them in Jamaica. Dolvis tried her best to calm her husband but he would not hear of it. He made a vow to cut Charmaine out of the will and banish her for life. Dolvis thought it best to leave it alone and allow him space to take it all in stride. However as soon as that storm was about to lift, I entered my party phase and started dating Larry a young man neither parent cared or approved of. The truth of the matter was we had been raised quite sheltered and there were few life lessons given to us by either of our parents. Their method was that of ignorance and celibacy. I was always a studious student more reserved and didn't care for much friends, but puberty changed all of that. It was my time to fly onto the social scene and get some street wise lessons. As a result as my sister before me I also found myself pregnant with child less than two years later. My dad took it hard and landed in the hospital with chest pains. It was not officially diagnosed but I am certain today it would be called stress pains.

It was a drastic change in my life experience as well as I was not prepared for this occurrence in my life at this point. I was enjoying my freedom to party but lacked the know how about birth control a topic that was foreign in my home. I struggled with the shame and the knowledge that I had disappointed my parents. So much so that I hid my pregnancy from them until I was in my sixth month and needed funds from my mother. It was then I made the dreaded call to her workplace to break the news. Dolvis I am sure knew but was also in denial and my honest confession of my impending condition of birth got a prompt click on the other end as she hang up the phone and took some time to deliberate rather than give me an angry response. I did later take consolation in the fact that my father always stated that he had a preference for raising girls. His motto was girls can bring a baby home, but boys will bring the police. Of the two evils he preferred the baby!!!

I chose to move in with my older sisters at this junction in my life to lessen the pain that my parents would have endured if they had to see me on a daily basis.

This indeed was an extremely stressful time for us as a family. It pays to mention here that abortion was not a reality even If I would have considered that option. My mother was a Christian and that was against her belief. It was also before the legalization of abortion in Canada. Some of my schoolmates at the time were doing illegal abortions in the States which were costly and not safe. Adoption was also a definite no. My mother would not allow me to give up her grandchild under any circumstances, period!!

After heads had cooled and I came to accept my fate, Dolvis agreed to help me with the care of my child on one condition that I must return to finish high school and go on to university. Those were her terms and I accepted them. Dolvis was an only child and she loved children. So, it was on August 20th, 1972 I had a son born 2 months premature. I found out afterwards that my mom had wanted to have a son. It was no wonder that she bonded so well with her two grandsons. Korey my sister's son and my son Khareme. Even Noel who had mostly daughters welcomed the change of little men running around the home. The early seventies brought a wind of change as Noel and Dolvis settled into this new phase of life as grandparents.

Dorothy and Lelieth had started the dream of higher education and were both enrolled in university. Lelieth was attending York, Erindale Campus and Dorothy University of Toronto.

The 70's opened up opportunities for many and everyone to afford higher education. Both UFT and York were expanding and hence needed students. Most applicants were accepted with C+ over at UFT but York which was a newer university and just starting to gain a reputation accepted students with even a D+ average. University costs back then were about $800 per year and far more affordable for students. Lelieth had worked part time throughout high school at Scarborough General Hospital and with some savings and help from the older sibling was able to pay fees and attend university. Dorothy had taken some time off to work full time and then decided to go back for her degree. Liz had enrolled in Seneca nursing program and was on her way to become a nurse.

The sacrifices had paid off and the younger children had taken flight to go for higher education and acquire skills and knowledge to improve their quality of life.

The year I had my son was the same year my brother Keith tied the knot with his fiancée of 2 years, Josephine. They had decided to live together and save for a home and got married as soon as that goal was achieved. Keith had maintained a good job at Honeywell with a good union over the years and was now ready to branch out with his own family. Keith started a trend then as the next year Liz finished and completed her nursing and became engaged at Christmas to her boyfriend Dunkley. Her wedding was the next summer of 1973.

Black pride and black power were now rampant during the seventies and my sisters and myself embraced this new ideology. We would wear our dashikis and most proudly started to let our natural hair by wearing the Afro. This created quite a stir in our home. Dolvis had little to say even though she silently liked and enjoyed our creativity, but Noel was hell bent on showing his distaste for our bushy hair and style of dress.

After a rather traditional wedding planned by Keith and his wife Josephine; the following year 1973, Liz's wedding took a dramatic turn to traditional

African style much to the disapproval of Noel. He was simply overruled by our zealousness and love of everything African. We all donned on the dashiki style gown for bride and bridemaids. Noel as the give-away father stuck to his traditional suit and tie and could not be encouraged to wear anything else.

The following year 1974 summer Lelieth also took the plunge into marriage and yes, another African style wedding. This time the very instrument symbolic of Africa the drums was used in the church as the bride made her entrance. Again, my dad was forced to comply to the wishes of his family. Lelieth was the mastermind and creative wedding planner in both weddings. Themes and design of wedding ensemble was her mastery. She had graduated that year from UFT and true to her revived cultural awakening and that of her new husband Patrick she set off to do her law degree at University of the West Indies in Trinidad. Patrick likewise went to Jamaica Mona Campus to study for his medical degree. Both had decided to return to Jamaica to live and practice with their new skills.

After 3 years of marriage flurry life for Dolvis and Noel it then became a birthing chamber as Keith had his first son, Liz also had her first son in a matter of 2 years and their grandchildren pool had expanded to four, all grandsons.

Here is pic of first grandson Korey at the age of 2 years. Korey just like his mom Charmaine was a pleasant happy child who loved food. Dolvis loved having him over as he was a joy to feed.

Here is a pic of all the early grandchildren and grand-nephew, all boys. The second genera-tion was proving to be a family of boys. From right we have Khareme, my son and the second grand child, then Yerodin, Lola's son. Next, we have in the background Kareem Ivy's son the grand-nephew., then Orande, Joy Elizabeth's son and Richard Keith's son farthest left.

Holidays were now a grand affair with the extended family group; so much so that we now had to start a new rule that we would only buy for the children and pick a name for the adults. Dolvis and Noel were very content with the new families that were now emerging and expanding. There were no more marriages on the agenda as Dorothy was still finishing up her degree at UFT Charmaine had finally settled down and returned to get her high school diploma after taking some time off after she had her son. I had completed high school and was now attending UFT working on my undergrad degree. Sharon was the only child still living at home, so it was now time for Noel to push his plans to return home to retire. Noel plans were to retire in 1977.

Sharon had started dating Howard seriously a local Jamaican young man working in the trades as a welder and even though a good student had let my parents know she wanted to work for a year prior to going to college. That was so she could pay her own way. At this point in time financially Dolvis was doing much better so Sharon the youngest did not have to contribute to the household. It was okay for her to save her funds to use for her intended goal of further studies. Noel and Dolvis had seen their children all embark on their own path and were becoming self-sufficient.

It was the mid-seventies and 3 daughters were married and had achieved higher education. Charmaine had also decided to pursue a nursing career after getting her high school diploma.

Sharon was now working in a bank as a customer service representative and saving for college. Keith was married owned his own home and now had a son and daughter. Total grandchildren count was now five. Four boys and I girl. Everyone was either working or in school furthering their education. The bumps and snags on the road were well worth their sacrifices.

It was probably because of the word sacrifice and duty so commonly used in the church sermons that might have caused Dolvis to cave and decide to forgo any other thought of staying in Canada. She now had to shift focus to prepare to embark on returning to Jamaica to retire and end her days. It was true that Noel had never been faithful as a husband to her during the marriage, but he had been there and had made the sacrifice for his children. Dolvis was now in her 50's and very old-fashioned. To start all over with another partner was just unthinkable. She was a trained dietician with years of experience so she would continue to work in Jamaica and allow her husband to enjoy his retirement. She had not worked long enough in Canada to get a comfortable retirement and neither had Noel so she would need to work for some time to maintain the lifestyle she wanted to live. Again, she had to ensure that she did not depend on the finances of a man that had truly never contributed fully to the household so she decided to also buy her own home in Jamaica as well to ensure her own financial well-being.

With the help of her stepfather Albert or Baba as he was fondly called, both Dolvis and Noel bought two government homes in May Pen, Jamaica. During the 70's the Jamaican government was encouraging home ownership so small homes were built and sold to Jamaicans at a nominal cost. These homes provided a basic 2-bedroom kitchen bathroom and living area. My parents did not see the homes and since I was making a trip to the island I was asked to visit and give feedback on my return to Canada. I was impressed with the awesome construction of the all-brick homes but was taken back by how small the homes were with no style in design. This I reported back to both Dolvis and Noel on my return. As I suspected this was not what my mother intended to live in on her return home. She was always known for thinking big and she wanted a home that would afford more space for the families to visit and for her to entertain.

Noel was of a different mind-set. Dolvis acted immediately on my report to sell that home and request Albert find another that would provide more space and a bit of luxury. Dolvis finally settled on getting two of those homes in St. Catherines side by side which she custom designed by asking the builder to combine the two homes to provide a five bedroom bungalow with 3 bathrooms, a large kitchen and 2 living room areas.

This was quite satisfactory for Dolvis as she and Noel would be able to live comfortable in separate rooms on one side with their own bathroom and leave the other three bedrooms for guests and family to visit. In planning for her retirement Dolvis was still quite cognitive of making sure she had room to have access to family and especially her grandkids visiting and spending some time.

There was still so much work to do in preparing and planning that move back to Jamaica. She would have to resign from her job at Scarborough General Hospital. This was a job that she loved and got a lot of love from as well. As on staff dietician over the years she was firm but respected and treated everyone with grace and style. I remember as a part time dietary aide how the student loved her and respected her. There were a few other dieticians that they detested strongly. Part of the reason was of course due to the habit of the students taking the extra food without approval. Some of the other dieticians where very rude to the students when they got caught taking food. Most of the part time teenagers came to work right after school and we were working in the kitchen putting food on the trays that went up to the patients. There was always too much food at the end of the day and the head girls who acted as runners would always look out for the supervisors and sneak the food to us so we could have a snack, especially when it was barbecued chicken legs and cakes and pies for dessert. Most of the leftover food would go to waste, but. yet it was not given to us so we would sneak and eat when and where possible. All the dieticians were aware of this and some including Dolvis did not go out of their way to police us as long as we have done our job well, the trays of food were checked and distributed to the patients in a timely manner.

Dolvis enjoyed the banter of young people and the excitement their energy brought to the dietary staff at the hospital. She would miss them, and they would miss her as well. Dolvis also got along famously with her co-workers and the head of the department. They would socialize together at most of the social gathering at the hospital. Her resignation had to be given and she knew they would have a small goodbye celebration for her. She would look forward to that. The other difficult task for her would be giving up taking care of the special-needs children. They had become like her children so she would need to find a replacement for them. She saw this as a wonderful opportunity to pass on this legacy to a family member, so she approached her daughter Joy to give her the first chance at his opportunity. Joy was very creative with a fetish for cleansiness and order. She had just returned from USA where she had stayed and worked in the stock market for 5 years. The stress of living without papers had taken its toll on her and when she suffered some health setbacks she decided to return to Canada. Dolvis had invested in a condo for her return and luckily her tenants had finally gotten a subsidized housing accommodation.

Joy was of course on her return very unhappy with the state of her condo and set about to clean and renovate and put her personal spin on things. Dolvis saw the opportunity for Joy who was still single and childless to have a home-based business taking care of these children. Dolvis approached Joy with this idea even though she knew this was most likely something that Joy would not do.

Joy lacked caregiving skills but as her first child it was the right thing to give her the opportunity to accept or decline. Joy declined her offer so Dolvis then suggested the idea to me. I was a single parent about to finish my degree program with a major in Sociology so she thought it might be a good fit. I also decided to pass on the idea as I did not yet have a clear vision as to what I wanted to do with this degree. Luckily for Dolvis Lola had also just returned from USA after a relationship that did not go well. She had also come back with child and Dolvis now had another grandson Yerodin. Yerodin was constantly in the hospital with asthma and Lola was not comfortable with leaving him to find work. Lola had spent years working as a health care aide and was the perfect fit for this home-based care giving. So, with the blessings of myself and Joy Lola took on this assignment and legacy from Dolvis. Lola did an awesome job with this opportunity. It allowed her to stay home and take care of Yerodin and make an honest living as well as a care giver for special needs children. Lola in fine style took this project on to new heights that Dolvis had not conceived by moving on to take on the emotionally challenged youth. This was truly her gifting and is so doing assisted and helped to transform the lives of many troubled youths that were lucky to be placed in her home.

Dolvis had one final task to accomplish before closing the chapter on her life in Canada and that was selling her home. She was fortunate to have the luck of the real estate market. Home prices skyrocketed in the mid 70's and her home that she had bought for a mere 30k was now worth over 100k. She was able to make a hefty profit that allowed her to buy her home in Jamaica mortgage free and have sufficient funds to ship all her belongings, furniture, and her beloved green Ford Toreno car to Jamaica.

The toll and stress of this move however came back to leave its mark on Dolvis. Her body was in the midst of menopause when all this was happening. She was forced to singlehanded manage, arrange, and finance this return trip back to her country of origin even though it was a move precipitated by Noel. Noel had left all planning and organizing in the capable hands of his wife and partner. Noel liked and enjoyed a stress-free life and as such was looking forward and instigated the move to Jamaica but as was his style he did not partake in the stress related planning and orchestrating of the move. As a result when the dust settled in Jamaica she was diagnosed with early diabetes which was a condition she was forced to manage for the remainder of her years and the very cause that eventually took her from us many years later.

Dolvis and Noel were content upon their return home to their homeland in the summer of 1977 in that their mission impossible had been made possible.

They had successfully launched ten children and numerous relatives and friends into Canada to seek a better life. Five of the ten children had achieved higher education and four were now gainfully employed with skills that were recognized in the industry. One was gainfully self-employed in the home care industry.

Sharon the baby of the family had taken a year off to work but during that year had become engaged to Howard a tradesman and welder by profession. She was also in good hands. The wedding was the same summer of 1977 of the retirement move to Jamaica, so Dolvis alone made the trip back with the blessings of Noel sent via his handwritten speech. This speech she was instructed to read verbatim at the wedding.

Some of the notable in our community that passed through the home of Dolvis and Noel included Joy and Winston Davis a young couple with amazing singing abilities. Joy was a high soprano and her husband Winston a solid bass tenor. They became a stable in our family functions, singing at all wedding and special events. Then there was Ronald and Faye Blake. Ronald went on to become a highly respected businessman who created and operated Higher Marks a tutoring school for children. Ronald excelled in the art of transforming those young children into great scholars. He also became our resident MC at all family and social events. Another notable in our home was Karl Fuller one of the early Director of the Jamaican Canadian Association. This community group was formed by Jamaicans in the early 1960's to help Jamaicans assimilate into life in Canada, and to also champion for their rights and create a social setting for them to interact and stay connected.

Their journey to Canada now complete Noel and Dolvis settled into retirement in their homeland of Jamaica. Dolvis was happy that the home was big enough to encourage the family to visit on holidays. As well three of their grandchildren accompanied them on their return trip home. Both Charmaine and I had just finished university and nursing college. I had just started a night job at Canada Post and could not find anyone suitable to babysit my son Khareme at night. Dolvis welcomed her grandson to stay in Jamaica to allow me to save and buy a car. Charmaine was also just starting out her nursing career and was also working night shifts so she also sent her two sons Korey and Khary to stay with grandparents in Jamaica. The circle of life continued for Dolvis and Noel. They were going home to retire but not without new tasks, one of which was to spend time with three grandsons teaching and providing them with the cultural norms and values of their motherland. This was a task that she welcomed as it kept her connected to her loved ones. The job of transferring skills to the younger generation was now in full force!!

Final pic is a pic of Dolvis and Noel on a return trip to Canada in 1982 for Lola's wedding in 1982. This is a rare pic of both of them together and depicts my dad looking affecticnately at my mom. Just another point in the complexities of a man and perhaps why my mom did decide to stay in her marriage as she saw and felt what was captured in this moment on camera.

WAISOME FAMILY TREE

||||||||||||||||||||||||||||||||||||||||||||||||||||||||||||||||||||||||||||||||||||||||||||||||||||||||||||

JAMES WAISOME & 1ST WIFE

(Her name is not remembered –
she died young believed to be poisoned for land)
They begat 7 children

ASTIN

Son went to Panama and all family trace was lost

MARY

Daughter: She had 3 children 2 boys and a girl. Their names were Timothy, Stanford and Florence

Timothy had a daughter Joyce-Joyce has 3 sons Calvin, Lloyd and Igal. Calvin has 3 children with his 1st wife and is currently divorced and at last count 4 additional children. Lloyd is married and has two children Matthew and Sarah. Igal also has two children.

Stanford-son-had 2 daughters Ena and Nana. Both Ena and Nana had children but the family lost contact and it is not known how many children they had.

Florence his only daughter did not have any natural children but did adopt a son and here again the family has lost touch with the whereabouts of this child.

TIMOTHY

Son-had one daughter Mavis. Mavis is now the oldest living Matriarch of the Waisome family and now lives in England. She had 7 children. Her oldest Janet lives in USA with her husband and has 2 daughters Sandra and Nichelle also living in the USA. Her second son Devon died some time ago from leuxemia. He had 3 natural children with his wife and 3 step-children. He now has at least 4 grandchildren. Her additional children are Pauline, Eaton. Colleen, Patricia and Hector.

She has at least 10 grandchildren and most of her family reside in England.

BERTHA

Daughter had one child a son who died and no record of any children.

STEPHEN

Son-was married twice and spent most of his life in Panama-1st wife name believed to be Emily who gave him 2 daughters Joan and Donna. Donna had 4 children 3 girls and a boy, one daughter Anne is living in England. Joan has no children and is living in Canada.

RUTH

Daughter-mother of Dolvis. -Dolvis had 4 natural children. Joy, Charmaine, Ingrid and Sharon, and 6 stepchildren, Norma, Keith, Lola, Dorothy, Joy and Lelieth.

Dolvis now has 4 natural grandchildren Korey, Khareme, Camara and Khary.and 8 step grandchildren Tamara & Shanta, Richard & Cheryl, Orande & Nathia, Kiwi, Jamilla, & Nashana. So far there are also 10 step-grandchildren.

AGNES

Daughter-had two children Winston and Ivy. Winston had 3 children and Ivy had 2 boys Donald and Kareem. So far there are at least 10 great grandchildren.

JAMES WAISOME AND 2ND WIFE

Had 2 Daughters Hilda and Ruby

Hilda had 4 children Vincent, Neville, Vendrice & Vernie. Hilda had over 10 grandchildren and great-grandchildren with the majority coming from Vincent.

Ruby had 2 children Millicent and Sample. Not sure of extended family as this family tree line over the years has lost contact with the main branch.

CHRISTMAS BLACK CAKE RECIPE

||||||||||||||||||||||||||||||||||||||||||||||||||||||||||||||||||||||||||||

This is my mom's recipe passed on to my sister Sharon who does a good job of baking black cakes.

Preheat oven to 350
- 1 lb butter or margarine
- 1 lb sugar
- 12 eggs
- 1 lb flour
- 2 teaspoon baking powder
- 1/2 teaspoon baking soda
- 4-5 tbsp browning or 1 cup molasses
- Flavouring which includes cinnamon, nutmeg, vanilla
- Rum ½ bottle
- Stout 1 pint
- Brandy 1 pint
- Fruits (mixture of raisins prunes, currants, lemon peel, cherries)
- 1 lb almond and walnuts

First it is best to blend all fruits in blender or food processor at least a month before baking. Add rum, stout and brandy and put in bottle or container to soak so that the fruits absorb the alcohol.

Cream sugar and butter until softened.

Add eggs and continue mixing. If possible remove eyes from eggs please do so to reduce raw taste in cakes. If not please add a teaspoon of lemon juice to cut rawness

Mix all dry ingredients which include flour baking powder, baking soda, nutmeg, cinnamon in a separate bowl

Slowly add to the creamed mixture. Also add vanilla

When mixture is combined slowly add molasses or browning to give colour to the cake

Add blended fruits with liquor slowly and mix thoroughly

Place in pans that have been buttered and floured.

At the bottom of oven place other pans with water to give extra moisture to baking process

Bake at 350 for about 45 minutes or until cake when pricked with a knife comes out clean.

NB for a heavier Wedding cake or Plum Pudding as it is more commonly called one needs to adjust and add more butter, flour and fruits to taste. That will result in a heavier cake with a texture more like a pudding.

ACKNOWLEDGEMENTS

||||||||||||||||||||||||||||||||||||||||||||||||||||||||||||||||||||||||||||||||||||||||||||||||||||||||||

First and four-most my thanks go out to my amazing mother Dolvis who took chances and in so doing set a remarkable example for myself and our family to pattern and live our lives. Next to my friend Patricia Tully who when I suggested for her to co-author with me on this journey into our mother's life, did not hesitate but replied yes, and added that she also had a goal to write her mother's story. It was this collaboration that kept me going at times when I got lazy and just did not feel like writing. Lisa as she is fondly called accepted the challenge and kept writing even when I had only managed to script a few pages.

To my family members Ivy Matthews who assisted me with the family tree and pictures of my mother; my sister Charmaine and her pictures and stories of mom; my son Khareme for his encouragement and support; my nephew Yerodin who also supplied family pictures and assisted with a walk down memory lane of his late mother and my sister Lola Barnes.

Thanks to my two stepdaughters, Reneasia and Reshauna who took on chores around the home in order to give me time and space to write undisturbed.

Thanks to the contributions of Nigerian Artist and Poet Uche Uwadinachi who was willing to donate his poetry and artistry to the evolution of this story, however; I knew my mom appreciated value and would want him compensated for his gifts and so that was negotiated in appreciation for his cover pencil art and poems which were added to the story. Uche also was the creator of our cover design for the book. Much appreciated!!!

Thanks to all who take the time to read, learn and evolve from this story. May your life be blessed and enriched for the better!!!

Finally, to God for giving me health and strength and determination to see this project through to the end. To define its purpose not only an act of love but as a legacy not only for my family but for the ethnic and immigrant community to use as a guide and learning tool.

BOOK 2

||||||||||||||||||||||||||||||||||||

VERONICA'S STORY

||||||||||||||||||||||||||||||||||||||||||||||||||

BY PATRICIA LOUISA TULLY

FOREWORD

||||||||||||||||||||||||||||||||||||||||||||||||||||||||||

This book is dedicated to, and in honour of the author's mother, the late Veronica Tully who was a pioneer in her own right. Veronica weathered many storms raising her six children while also dedicating herself to love and care for so many others who cross her path.

The author, Patricia Tully, even as she herself had to overcome several challenges in life, was still able to elevate herself to the highest degree possible.

Her new book will show some of her skills in writing and the love she bore for her mother and family. As a multi-talented individual, writing is only one small part of her successes.

It took several months to research her book as she turned to family, friends and acquaintances for information, mostly long forgotten by some.

Her friends meant so much to her that she never failed to talk about them with honesty and love. Such attributes will be apparent in her new book.

It is with much pleasure that I write this Foreword in support of Patricia Tully as she is now fulfilling the long-time dream of honouring her mother.

Patricia expresses some of her innermost feelings in this book with candor and without many reservations.

Yvonne Ineta Weston

SECOND FOREWORD

||||||||||||||||||||||||||||||||||||||||||||||||||||||||||||||||| ||||||||||||||||||||||||||||||||

This beautifully written memoir is truly engrossing, and a pleasure to read. The author (Lisa Tully) interweaves personal story, family history, moral arguments, and executes them seamlessly with unblinking honesty. She presents the biography of a loving mother, saintly, but determined in her pursuits to tackle many existential issues to ensure a better life for her children. The story is truly inspiring.

In this powerful memoir, Lisa relates with poignancy, how her Mom, a teacher at 19 years of age, loses her first job because of the pregnancy of her firstborn son (Patrick). The irony is that this son, later in life became "an indispensable help line" to her Mom and siblings. Lisa skillfully manages with wit and humour, to show the reader how her Mom, with an indomitable spirit, and a positive attitude, pursued different occupations; got married then separated from her husband (her dad) after 8 years, and was left to care for her six children as a single parent. A native of Antigua, Veronica emigrated to U.S.A.; then to Canada in 1962 in search of a better life. Her struggle for survival commences, as challenges in her life intensify.

Buckle up! Notwithstanding the struggle she faces, Veronica rises to become one of the heroines of our times. Depicted as a woman of courage; an emblem of hope, fully propelled by love for all and malice for none, she displays strength and an undaunted spirit as she pursues her goal. These characteristics illuminate the pages as you read her story. Evidently, to know her was to love her, and Lisa has convincingly captured her personality on these pages.

A powerful and compelling read: Lisa relates the story of her family dynamics. Furthermore, Lisa provides a look into the social history of the past. You become riveted as she describes the goodness and relatedness of everyone on this lovely island of Antigua: their neighborly lifestyle, their kindness, caring, and responsibility for each other; their assumed roles for disciplining children, should they misbehave: the latter a replica of how it takes a Village to raise the child. Done nowadays, it will not be regarded as an entertaining delight.

Brilliantly and soberly written, you are captured by this humane story: The author's use of colloquial terms in true Caribbean style to convey meanings (seldom used nowadays) is refreshing: e.g." Picknee": meaning child; "Bakkra": meaning white people; "licks": meaning corporal punishment to someone who misbehaved; "Massa" meaning your boss.

Occasionally, you are introduced to traumas which beset Veronica, e.g. The death of her mother; her husband; her favorite sons Patrick, and Clayton. You are also introduced to ceremonial functions Veronica attended, and her impact on those she met. She was regarded as a butterfly that thrived; never sparing a moment; spreading her wings to do good to others; or tell you how much she loves you. This, despite the difficulties she faced.

Lisa narrates light-heartedly, how her Mother expanded her family: She lovingly embraced foreign students in Canada; Prime Minister; Governor General; the Homeless, among others. Veronica was the embodiment of love, goodness, compassion, kindness, and generosity. Her presence lifted your spirits and she encouraged everyone to" do good". Her tenacity even as she approached her ninety second birthday was remarkable; and her trust in God unshakeable.

In sum, this book is a compelling read as the author traces her mother's geographic journey from Antigua to Canada and back to Antigua. It explores the hard choices she had to make throughout her life. Apparently, the decisions she made were beneficial to her family, and those who had the privilege of knowing her were enriched by the experience. What makes the memoir so interesting to read is the wonderment of life and fate that informs every page. Veronica stands out as a luministic example of enlightenment and courage, and an emblem of hope. Without a doubt, to know her, was to love her.

Please read the book, and if you like it like I do, recommend it to others.

Adopted Picknee. Toronto, March 6, 2020.

DEDICATION

||||||||||||||||||||||||||||||||||||||||||||||| |||||||||||||

This book is dedicated to the memory of my dear Mother Veronica Elizabeth Adams Tully who has shaped me into the Woman I am. You will never be forgotten. "Love and Gratitude"

CHAPTER 1

||||||||||||||||||||||||||||||||||||||||||||||| ||||||||||

COUNTRY OF BIRTH
AND HISTORY

The beautiful island of Antigua – one of the Leeward Islands in the Caribbean – is where my precious mother, Veronica Elizabeth Adams, was born to Louisa Audain and Thomas Adams on February 5, 1920. She was also known as "May Adams" and had the features of her Father.

Louisa Audain, Veronica's Mother was born in Puerto Rico, between 1877 and 1880, of a Puerto Rican mother and an Antiguan father. Her Father was a seaman who had a light brown complexion and was always travelling up and down the islands. Her mother, meanwhile, was light-skinned and of Portuguese descent.

When her mother died in Puerto Rico, Louisa was only one year old. Her father then brought the child to his family in Antigua, where his sister raised her. But by the time she was five years old, her father died at sea and she became an orphan. It is said that her father had other children in the island of St Vincent whom she never met.

This was when Britain ruled the island, and the Blacks worked in the sugarcane and cotton fields. The master (massa) was king and, being white, was referred to as a "bakkra" by the natives. Children were called "picknee."

The British planters produced sugar and rum here on an island plagued by hurricanes and fires. The Black workers suffered harsh treatment and shockingly poor working conditions, which continued into the first half of the 20th century.

According to the biography *To Shoot Hard Labour* (Smith & Smith): *Antigua, as with all others in the British Empire, was a colony. Antiguan slaves were emancipated in 1834, but remained economically dependent upon the plantation owners.*

Economic opportunities for the new freedmen were limited by a lack of surplus farming land, no access to credit and an economy built on agriculture rather than manufacturing. Poor labour conditions persisted until 1939 when a member of a royal commission urged the formation of a trade union movement....

Among the many nationalities and ethnicities that settled, over time, on the island were the Irish. *The Irish were used by the British as a buffer group between them and the African slaves and became overseers on sugar plantations on the island. Many of the Irish had children with the Africans, which is why many Antiguans and Barbudans have Irish surnames to this day,* such as Tully.

... The colonial hierarchy gradually began to come apart as a result of universal education and better economic opportunity. This process gave rise to Africans reaching the highest strata of society and government.

The Antigua Trades and Labour Union, formed shortly afterward, became the political vehicle for Vere Cornwall Bird, who became the union's president in 1943. The Antigua Labour Party (ALP), formed by Bird and other trade unionists, first ran candidates in the 1946 elections and became the majority party in 1951, beginning a long history of electoral victories.

After slavery people lived in shanty towns and worked as labourers, and sugarcane production was the primary economy for over a century and up until 1939, when the Antigua Trades and Labour Union was formed... .

My uncle, Samuel James Sr., and my father, Walter Leslie Tully, became part of this union.

The estate owners were brutal in all the villages that were set up. The Blacks had no medical attention and the wages were the absolute minimum – less than it had cost to feed, clothe, and shelter the slaves.

Louisa became a worker for an estate owner, the famous Alexander Moody Stuart, then became a cook and, later, cooked for the men who worked on the American Air Force Base.

In those days, children belonged to the Massa and took his name, rather than the surnames of the men who fathered them. Education was attained through the Methodist Church at Gilberts Estate, when they were allowed to attend. There, one learned to write his name, sing *God save the Queen*, and was taught some religious verses.

CHAPTER 2

||||||||||||||||||||||||||||||||||||||||||||||||||||||||||

THE ROOTS

After Louisa Audain grew up surviving this kind of living, she had four children: one son and three daughters, of whom my Mom was the third child. The first was her son, Theodore H. Finch, followed by Delores *aka* Deli, then May/Veronica my Mom and Agatha. Louisa then married Horatio Buckley of St. John's.

Mom's father, Thomas Adams, hailed from the village of New Winthorpes in the Parish of St. George. He was a carpenter and also a minister for the Seventh Day Adventist Church. Mom was raised in the city, St. John's, with her maternal siblings, but she also had a brother and sister on her father's side.

Mom's younger sister, Agatha, who was known to be a very bright, beautiful and a pretty girl, died suspiciously. As the story goes, she was burned to death in what was believed to be an act of obeah/voodoo/black magic. Someone set a trap for her and she died mysteriously – in a fire that was not evident anywhere else but on her. People said that not even smothering her in heavy clothing could stop the fire and save her life. ...

Mom related to me that she remembers as a young girl spending time in Dominica and some areas in the town that she visited.

As a young girl, Mom was bright, friendly, outgoing and possessed a spirit of independence and the drive to accomplish and achieve.

It was difficult back then, growing up poor with parents who worked very hard for very little compensation from the Massa. So Mom learnt to be self reliant and self sufficient early in life, and this sustained her throughout her life and into her nineties.

Mom recounted stories of herself arguing with her brother Theodore as children. She recalled that, one time, he pestered her about being smarter than she was, and, in return, she began to mimic him, because he used to stammer. She told him he could barely make a sentence and continued to mock him by stammering. Furious with his sister, Theodore went for a knife, and she had to run for her life. He got a good licking for it, Mom told me.

Mom attended the St. John's Girls School, which was then located on East Street and Queen Elizabeth Highway, right across from the two Country Ponds. As a bright student, she had ambitions to attend the T.O.R. Memorial High School (or Miss Robinson School, as it was also called), one of the first established private schools. But Mom was not allowed. She was not light skinned or from the right kind of family, to start, and, in addition, her mother could not afford to send her to that school. The family for whom her mother worked was supposed to help them financially, but that never happened.

Mom's first job in her working career was as a teacher, even though she was very talented in dress making, at the very institution she attended – St. John's Girl School – until she was 19 years old. That is when she became pregnant with her first child – after having sex for the first time. Unmarried and pregnant, she could no longer teach because it was not allowed.

She said her older brother, Theodore, who was then the overseer for Mr. Warneford, the owner and massa of all of Yeptons Estate, was very put out and angry with her. Meanwhile, he had already fathered two children, a girl and a boy, with one woman whom he did not marry, and had a third child on the way with a different woman.

Nevertheless, Mom named her firstborn, a boy, after her brother, Theodore. The baby's middle name was Patrick, which is what he was always called. He was born eleven days after her twentieth Birthday. Patrick's father "took responsibility" and supported his child as best he could, with the help of his family, and then he migrated to New York and married someone else there.

Mom then concentrated on raising her child and her career as a Seamstress. She made really nice clothes for her clients and her children, wedding attire for brides, and bridesmaid's dresses.

Her older sister Delores, aka Aunt Deli, married Neville Fenton, and she had no children of her own; but her husband had a few whom she raised. She was a diabetic and fell sick with gangrene of the foot and ended up in the hospital. When the doctors wanted to operate and take her leg off she refused, and then she died. That was my second burial as a child. (My third was Aunt Emily, my Uncle Harold's wife, and the other was my uncle, Percival Gordon, my Aunt Avril's husband.)

After five years, Mom had her second child, another boy, who looked exactly like her, but had his father's complexion and tall slim body; she named him Lloy. Then, two years later, she had another child, her first daughter, named Joan Penelope.

When Joan was a toddler, Mom and my father met and then they started courting. My parents used to go out and have fun at the "talkies," now known to us as the movies, at parties, and dancing, and had many friends whom they socialized with including Sidney "Basenote" Thomas, Uncle Clem Walker and Godfather Carlton Weatherill and their families. Dad would also tow Mom on his bike; Granny was there to care for the children when Mom was out.

My father, Walter Leslie Tully, was the son of Molly Davis and Leslie Tully. He was born on May 8, 1916, and had two other siblings on his Mom's side, Harold and Avril. His mother, Molly, was the daughter of Georgiana Elvira "Ma Lady" Tomlinson-Davis and Matthew George Davis of Newfield Village. Molly and Ultima were twins, and their other children were Clayton, Jacob and Miriam Davis. His mother was sent away to St. Lucia, where, we are told, she had other children. So Dad and his siblings were raised by his maternal grandmother Georgiana Elvira "Ma Lady" Tomlinson-Davis. Dad also had a younger brother on his father's side: Kendrick Tully. Their father migrated to the United States when they were toddlers and there he married and had other children.

Dad never had any children until he met Mom and, two years later, they had their first child together, a son, whom Dad named Clayton Leslie Aliston Tully: Clayton after his uncle and Leslie after his father and himself. Clayton was also born on the same date as his older brother Harold.

Mom and Dad were married at St. George's Anglican Church in Fitches Creek in 1947. Mom's full name was Veronica Elizabeth Adams. But Dad said her name was too long and she should shorten Elizabeth to Elise, which she did from their wedding day forward. Unfortunately, they separated in 1955. But Dad lived in the same area as we did – just a three-minute walk down the road – and we saw him every day. He stopped by to hail us up in the morning on his way to work; and then again at the end of the day, he visited with us before going to his own residence.

As children, we grew up living with our grandmother Louisa Audain-Buckley, Mom's mother, who lived on Dickenson Bay Street (aka Back Street) in St. John's.

Mom had converted from the Anglican Church where she was christened and Moravian Church where she attended with Dad and became a born-again Christian at the Pilgrim Holiness Church (aka Mission Church) on Popeshead and Bishopgates Streets prior to my birth. We were raised as Christian children and had Sunday-morning worship at home, singing and praying before going to church and Sunday school.

In fact, we attended three Sundays Schools each Sunday: Moravian, Pilgrim and Mr. Crosby's Sunday school, which was located at the Hill Secondary School on Popeshead Street. And we had to know all the "Golden Texts" from each Sunday school, or we would "get licks," a beating with a belt, in addition to punishment.

Our house was uniquely built and had three differently shaped roofs. A smaller house in the yard was occupied by a Barbudan man and his family. Our home was on the north side of the street, situated between Popeshead Street and Wapping Lane, a couple of houses down from what was known as Miss Browne Corner.

Dad's sister, Avril Gordon, and her family lived very close by and Dad's brother, Harold Scholar, also lived nearby, on another street going further north. Then Dad's aunt, his Mother's twin Sister Ultima Davis-Hilman, lived a street over from us, on St. George's Street, and my cousin Victor lived with her.

We all called our great-grand aunt "DaDa." She unfortunately became blind, but she was very aware and smart, and you could not fool her, especially with money. If she sent you to the shop to purchase something, she knew exactly the amount you were supposed to bring back; and she would feel the circumference of the coin and know exactly what it was. Back then, it was "pound, shilling and pence," as we were a British colony.

Mom's siblings also lived close by. Her brother George Adams and sister Eunice Adams-Hamilton lived in the same area, a few streets over to the west and north of us on Alfred Peters Street, near Mom's friend, Mrs. Agnes Hurst. Our community was a village, with all our family and friends. Directly across the street from our home was my Mom's best friend, Jean Evanson/Aunt Jean, who was our family, and all the other adults in that home. They helped to raise us, including Nurse Cole, who was the midwife that assisted at all our births; and there was another neighbour in that household named Ivy Tittle.

Mom's friends and Christian sisters were Aunt Olive Christian, who lived further down Back Street. Aunt Olive raised her twin niece and nephew, Janet and Robert Henry, and Natalie and Vellie. Not forgetting Miss Oliver. We all grew up together like family. Mom, Aunt Jean, Aunt Olive, and Miss Oliver would be seen on Sundays with their long-sleeved dresses, hats, purses and Bibles in hand going to church at Pilgrim Holiness.

Wilmoth Daniel, his brother Samuel and Sister Ronnie first lived below the Gilliards' shop on the same side of the street as our home; and then they relocated right across the street from us. We all grew up together. Wilmoth was good friends with my brothers, Clayton and Walton, and Ronnie and my sister Joan were very good friends.

Below the Gilliards were Mrs. Corolita Erskine and her daughters, Nalda and Peaches; then Aunt Jim Foster with her family – William (Sonny), Bernice (George), Helen (Cutie), and Janis (Dotsie) Aunt Jim was my Brother Walton's Godmother and that made her Godmother to the rest of us; then the Poxsons, Maude and her husband, a policeman we called "Sergeant" and their daughter Molly; then Narna Withy's house; and then our home.

We had distinctive landmarks in our neighbourhood. Across the street from our house was a very big stone, like a bench, and we called it the "Roller." The adult used to sit on it and converse, especially in the evenings and at night; and behind that was a stand-pipe and then the big gutter. On that same side of the street, but further east, was the top "bathroom," where people would go to have a shower, boys and men, in particular.

On Wapping Lane and St. George's Street there were other shops: Mr. Joseph and J. D. Simon & Sons' rum shop – owned by Paddy Simon (the Griot) family – and at Back Street and Wapping Lane, right on the corner, we had Miss Tiny shop. We would be sent to the shop to buy food ingredients in small amounts, like butter, fat meat, cooking oil, flour, cornmeal, onions, etc., to cook dinner; and the adults would wrap the money in a piece of paper on which the items we needed were written. Sometimes, on the way to the shop, we would see our friends playing, and stop to play with them, and lose the money. That was serious, and we would get licks for sure. People didn't have money to lose, waste, or spend frivolously.

Sometimes children were not given any money, since parents would have a "trust"/credit account with most of the shops in the area. Then when they were sent to buy things, the shopkeeper added the bill to the family's account. It would be paid at the end of the week or month.

... At the corner of Popeshead and St. George's Streets was Miss Mussington's shop. She was my Godmother, and her nephew Ervin and my older brothers were friends and Janice and my sister Joan were also friends. In our family, most of us shared the same Godparents – like Uncle Clem Walker and Godfather Carlton Weatherill – and we grew up believing they were relatives, when they were really our parents' friends.

We were taught to respect our elders, which could be anyone older than you, including your siblings. You had to say "Good morning" to your neighbours and all "big people/adults" in general. Even if neighbours didn't talk with each other, and maybe had a disagreement, you – as a child – had nothing to do with it and still had to say "Good morning," or you would get a scolding if not licks.

Everybody knew each other and we lived together as family, with love, trust, and respect and shared lots of things. When relatives came into town from the country, with fruits and vegetables, we would share with the neighbours. My Granny always did.

When you went out to town, or wherever, and left your clothing on the line to dry and it looked like it was going to rain, your neighbour would pick up your clothes and take them into your home. And if your house was locked, which was seldom, and then they kept your things in their home until you got back.

Our neighbours could discipline us if we were rude or disrespectful; or if they saw us doing something wrong, they could, and did, beat us with a belt. Then they would tell our parents about it and we would get licks again from our parents at home. Teachers in school would discipline with a belt, also; and, again, when we got home, there would be another licking. It made us who we are today, since it did not kill us. We had Police in our community two doors away from us "Apache" Williams and Sargeant Poxson whose presence alone helped to keep us in line and respectful.

My Brother Clayton used to do his badness then run from licks, Mom had a hard time catching him, because he would run down the street to our father and sometimes under the house or the bed so Mom would put up all his licks until she can catch him good, when he runs under the bed she would use the broom stick to dig him out it used to be funny.

CHAPTER 3

|||||||||||||||||||||||||||||||||||||||||||||||||||| |||||||||||

HOW WE WERE BROUGHT UP

My brothers went to Moravian School, Point School and then to St. John's Boys School, while my sister went to the Moravian School, Faith and Hope High School (aka Miss Goodwin School) and then to Princess Margaret Secondary School. I went to a school up at "Mungo Tung," at the top of North Street, as a child, then on to Moravian School, and then to Faith and Hope High School. In those days, some children went to school without shoes on their feet, determined to get an education.

Back then, when you were a born-again Christian you had to wear long-sleeved clothes and your dresses past your knees, since women and girls were not allowed to wear shorts or pants, or make-up, or jewelry; and your hair had to be worn natural, with no "ironing" or chemical straightening. We were brought up very strict and disciplined, especially my Sister Joan and I.

While my siblings had been christened as babies in the Anglican and Moravian Churches, I was baptized in the Pilgrim Holiness Church by Pastor Taylor. There were two brothers – Ira and Wingrove – who were ministers at that church back then.

Our home had a flower garden at the front and on the left of the steps leading to the front door, and in our backyard we had fruit trees, including a dumps tree; a clothes line and a stone heap; and our property was fully fenced with a gate. We grew up with chickens, guinea pigs, rabbits, pigeons, ducks, dogs and a cat in our back yard, which boasted a rabbit coop and fowl coop.

My older brother Lloy would go looking for food for the rabbits and the guinea pigs. He also had a gym in the yard, where his friends would work out, doing body building, lifting weights, and doing repetitions on the pulley and so on.

We grew up on the best fruits: guavas, plums, golden apples, soursop, tamarind, cherries, mangoes, coconuts, pawpaw, sugar-apples, dumps, finger rose, bananas, sugarcane, seaside grapes and Barbuda coco plum, just to name a few. And for sweets, we had sugar cakes, fudge, tamarind stew, Miss Blackie's ice-cream, and Archie's flake-o/shaved ice/snow cone.

Archie lived on St. George's Street and we shared the same backyard fence. Next door to him were "Mama Sista" and Arnold, and they had a shop and a "jukebox." Part of our back fence was shared with them, too. I recall one day after Mom returned from America she was doing her worship, I was about eight or nine years old and I was in the yard by the kitchen which was pretty close to our back fence and the "benna" music was playing, it was really sweet and I was there winning up my little self and having a good time making up some moves and feeling happy with myself, the next thing I realize Mom was at the bedroom window looking at me behaving like this, I was frightened/shocked and scared and yes, she gave me a good licking for that, what we call "cut arse" and with every lick the words were spoken, I am raising you to be a decent and Christian person and you behaving like a vagabond, and where you know how to do that.

As children, we played with each other and had many games: skipping, hopscotch, dolly-catcher, and hand games, marbles, cashew, rounders, and cricket, fly kites etc. On moonlight nights we sat on the steps and told stories until we were too scared to even move – jumby/ghost stories and "Brer Anancy" stories with my friend who lived east of us, with her siblings, her mom, and her granny. We played with the Ryans, Joycie and Alexis, while Jackie and my sister Joan were friends as well. They lived a couple houses to the west of us before moving to Wapping Lane, closer to Alfred Peters Street.

We were well socialized, as we interacted with each other on a daily basis. We created our own games and made kites, tops, scooters, and so much more. We made our own bats and stumps for cricket and invented things to do. At the beach, we floated on tires and dagger logs. We would dare each other – for example, knock this leaf, paper, stone or whatever from my shoulder. But it never escalated into anything serious or using weapons on each other. It was easy to resolve situations; conflict resolution was not a problem.

Before going to bed at night, we had to brush our teeth and "wash off," especially us girls, and wash our underwear (we were not taught to pile them up for days and then wash them.) And we had to wash our feet also. Granny would say that mice would nibble at our feet if we didn't.

Girls in the community used to go to the home of Miss Graham, the seamstress, to learn "needle work" – that is, to sew by hand first then on the sewing machine. She lived west of us. And on the other side of the street lived Pat White and his family; and to the east, Miss Chrissie; and to the west was Mr. Tanner.

Mom was a supervisor/community leader, and during the summer she would take us and all the children from our street – the Blanchettes, the Gilliards, the Daniels, and many others – to the beach in the early morning, down to "Washan Basin" near Rat Island, at the bottom of Back Street. We loved it and had a lot of fun.

Dad used to play the pools, the Irish sweepstakes in England, and he used our names on them. One month, he won a lot of money on the sweepstakes that carried my Brother Walton's name on it. As an investment and to assist in providing for his children – as he and Mom agreed – he had a house built on Fort Road, right across from Percival's Gas Station. It was a unique house at the time, with a gallery all around it.

Although it was built for us, we never lived in it. First, it was occupied by Dad's favourite nephew Winston, right after he got married, he moved in with his wife, and they started their family while living there for a few years. Then the Pigott family rented and occupied it for many years.

Dad was an artist and sign painter, and so was his Brother Ken Tully, and they would work together on projects – some for construction companies and designing and painting the Carnival stage. Uncle Ken always served on the Carnival Committee with the Shouls, Ms. Yvonne Maginley, and others. Dad also worked at a place called Tomlinsons for many years.

Dad was the opposite of Mom: He played Mas' at Carnival time and was always on one of the floats he helped to create. I recall my siblings and I, and my Cousin Essie, Aunt Martha's son, who was also raised with us like our brother, being with our Granny on the landing of Mr. Pestaina's store, at the corner of

Popeshead and St. John's Streets, where the Carnival parade turns to go into the Point Area. I was only six, seven and eight years old at the time.

As my brothers got older, they were allowed to play Mas'. Well, Dad took them to play Mas' because they wanted to; but it was not authorized or sanctioned by Mom. She was never pleased and argued with our Dad about it. She was raising Christian children who did not participate in such things, she said.

I recall being a little envious of my friend Valerie Harris, in particular, when I would see her in the parade as a majorette. I would stand there wishing I could be doing that, too, and so did my sister when she would see her school friends participating in Carnival.

Dad was also a fix-it man, especially of bicycles, which he also painted. They were his mode of transportation, because he was a drinking and card-playing man. At his home, he used to run a joint, where men gathered and played games and drank. They played dominos and card games, in particular.

Dad was very good at card games, particularly at playing bridge; and he has trained many and some of the best bridge players the island has produced – including my cousin the late Duncan Finch, Alexis Mathurin, and King Frank-I. They have played in tournaments around the world, winning champion trophies for Antigua and Barbuda.

After Mom and Dad separated, she then changed careers from being self employed to working in Maurice Michael's clothing store on Market Street/Scots Row, making $16.00 each week which she did for over a year. The store sold fabrics and all the trimmings, and the workers would measure the cloth and cut according to the customers' requirements. Mom was very good at it, matching the right thread, zippers, buttons, lining, lace, etc. Since she was a skilled seamstress with the necessary experience, she would guide the patrons on how to coordinate what they were going to make.

The customers would come into the store and always ask for the Christian lady to attend to them. She made all types of friends, including a man named "Hash Rider," who would say to her, "If nearga trubble you and you picknee and dem, jus tell me." In other words, if anyone interfered with her and her children, she should let him know.

Mom was very good at reading and loved to read, and I can never forget an experience she had back then, which she shared with me. The newspaper was delivered to the store for Mr. Michael, and when not busy she would read it.

One day Mr. Michael ordered her, in the presence of everyone, to put down his newspaper. He said she could not read it before him, because it was *his* paper; and if she did it again she would pay for the paper. He ordered her to find some work to do, sweeping and cleaning the store.

It was hurtful for her and embarrassing. She felt very small and like nothing, as he "put her in her place" this she related to me. That experience taught her a real lesson, making her super strong, independent, and self reliant, and it gave her determination and impetus that propelled her to set goals to accomplish, and never *ever* to be spoken to like that again. She told me when you work for people you have to put up with their rules and sometimes insults, disrespect and injustice which was not right, and not fair.

Mom then found a better paying job at one of the first hotels in Antigua. It was not exactly a hotel, but an exclusive millionaire's club called the "Mill Reef Club" located on a beach on the east coast in the parish of St. Philip.

It was during this period, I recall, that our grandmother got sick and then died. This was the only grandparent I knew, and I am named Louisa after her. By the time I came along, the only grandparent left was my Granny. We, the younger ones, were always with our Grandmother. My two older brothers immediately ahead of me and my younger brother/cousin Ellsworth, aka Essie, we went everywhere with Granny, especially me. I was very close with my Granny, and she had some pet names for me including "dodo darling, Loulou, and Louwe." Granny called Mom "May and May ann" she never called her Veronica.

When we went to Pigotts to see my cousins, we would first stop off at Miss Addie's shop and visit with her, then continue into the village by Uncle Joshua, and Aunt Henrietta James, and then we would go up to Uncle Sammy and Aunt Mary James' home. Also, we used to go with Granny to the top of St. Mary's Street and visit some old ladies, who, I believe, were Portuguese, like Miss O'Fleck. I think they were related to Granny. We also went to Blizzard and Winthorpes Village to visit her cousins, Merle and her mother, and Mom's father's family.

I used to go with Granny to her Women's Lodge meetings on Newgate Street, upstairs Masses House, just west of where the Antigua & Barbuda Workers Union is located now. The members used to have me perform and do recitations, and my friend Valerie Harris and her sister Brenda used to perform, as well. They also attended with their grandmother.

In those days, grannies were "old ladies" and they were very good caretakers of their grandchildren. They wore big, long skirts and dresses and tied their heads most of the time. The Women's Lodge wore a lot of white dresses and a rosette, especially for official functions.

My granny was very kind and loving, and very affectionate; she loved kisses and we were taught to always greet each other with a kiss. If we came home and did not kiss Granny, she sent us back out of the house "until you find your manners."

Every Sunday she cooked lots of food and would feed the neighbours: Narna Withy directly east of us; Narna for Ownley/Rose; and Mem, another old lady who lived east of us, by the alley that led to St. George's Street. West of us there was Thomas' mother in the bigger of the two houses, while he occupied the smaller one that was always on a portion of our land. And in front of them and west of us were Mother Joe, the Joseph family, George "Nugget" Joseph, and his children with whom we used to play.

We grew up seeing how families cared for our elders until they died, like my Mom did with her mother, our granny. It was our basic culture: We did not put our grandparents or any elderly person in nursing homes. In fact, those places did not even exist back then.

We took the elders meals on a daily basis, breakfast, lunch and dinner. Some children had to do this every day before going to school: take breakfast and, sometimes, lunch at the same time for their grandparents or relatives. A thermos was used for the tea, and there was a particular utensil – a "carrier" – that had three levels of containers in which the food was placed, and a handle, which was used for the delivery of the meals.

My siblings and I – and others like Rigsdale, Pops, and Essie – were given food from Aunt Jean and Miss Tittle and Godie Nurse to take to "Ann Des," who lived on the opposite side of the street, at the rear of the bathroom on that side, below Mr. Blackett's house, and that was part of our daily living and routine.

As children, we got up early in the mornings, and some children had a lot of chores to do before going to school. I have heard a few of my older cousins talk about taking care of animals first thing in the morning, with goats, sheep and cows to tie out, feed, and sometimes milk. These animals were their parents' livelihood and their means to provide for the family.

If we were poor, we didn't know it, because we were never hungry. I don't know that we wanted anything or lacked for anything. I was a picky and slow eater, and my brothers would steal my food. They would distract me and take my meat from my plate, and sometimes I would cry; but I soon learned and protected my food from them.

We had to eat what was provided for us and be thankful. But it was always good local food: provisions, rice, meats – goat, lamb and beef, fowl/chicken, salt fish, red herring, shad, fish – with fungie, pepperpot, ducana, corn meal porridge, rice porridge, white dumplings, potato dumplings, bread and cheese, corn beef, noodles, and lots of milk, bush tea, and cocoa tea, and tons of fruits and vegetables. Then they gave us cod liver oil, Marmite, and senna for a good clean-out. We had it all.

Granny did not have to discipline by beating us; if we were misbehaving she would give us that particular look with her eyes alone, and we knew to straighten up and behave ourselves. Essie was very stubborn and he and the boys would get into trouble. Then Granny would hold Essie by his ear and pull on it, telling him he was too "harden," and that "who nar hear ah go feel," meaning he did not listen and he would feel the consequences of not listening and doing as he was told. She taught us not to trouble things that didn't belong to us and not to lend or borrow people things, make do with what you have, till you can do better.

Granny and Mom taught us to be loving and kind with each other and everyone. Whenever we had disagreements and fights, we had to hug and kiss and make up. Granny did not make skylark/joke with that, and Mom was worse.

My granny could balance a bucket or a basket on her head. First, she put on her catta/head tie (she loved head ties and hats and always wore them), and then she would put a bucket of water from the stand pipe on her head and then in each hand.

She had the nicest skin, smile, and hands, and I loved being in her lap and hiding from my brothers behind her, wrapped up in her big skirt. I used to love to play with her hair; it was long and very soft with a wavy kind of curl to it.

Granny had a cat and he knew how to find Granny, when we were coming home he would come to the top of Back Street by Deanery and meet Granny.

I also recall the day when my uncle Theodore Finch and Aunt Dada, his wife, visited when Granny was sick. She said to him and my Daddy that "Mama no look good; she going," about my grandmother. I left the house with them and we went down the road to my Dad's house. We had just gotten there when Clayton came running breathing hard and said, "Mommy say to come cause Granny gone."

I didn't love my aunt too much after that, since she had caused my granny to die. I was not eight years old as yet, and I didn't quite get it. I just did not understand how and why. I did not expect Granny to go anywhere and leave me; I thought she just did not feel good and that she would get better soon. When we got back to our house, my siblings and Aunt Martha were there and everyone was crying, plenty bawling and hollering, particularly by my Mom, and I remember neighbours and people coming to our home.

Back then, most of the dead were laid out in their home until the funeral. The undertaker, Mr. Straffie from Fort Road, came to our home to embalm Granny's body; however, for me, he did stuff to her body that I did not understand. I was being disobedient and was peeping by pulling the curtain at the bedroom window when she was laid out in the living room. I was supposed to be in bed sleeping, but I could not sleep, and I thought he was hurting her. Mommy and Daddy finally explained to me that Granny was no more; she didn't feel anything; and she had gone to Heaven in the skies. They did allow me to comb her hair, stroking it with my hands for the last time. Her cat went and lay on her belly as she was laid out in the Living room. Afterwards he used to moan all the time.

At the funeral Granny's Lodge women were present, and all our family, and then we went to the grave yard. This was devastating for me, especially when they put her in that hole and Mommy started to wail and bawl, trying to go in the hole, too. There I was, hanging onto her, because I wanted to go into the hole with her, as well; Mom was not leaving me too, this was very bad I knew that and it was pain which I didn't like. Then Brother Pat, Daddy, Aunt Jean, Goddy Nurse Cole was holding on to Mommy pulling her up and back from the dark deep hole Granny's box went down.

In those days, the funeral procession was mainly people walking behind the hearse to the church and to the cemetery. It did not take very long since the burial ground was in close proximity to the town. The best transportation, back then, was our feet, which we called "AG 2" – like the vehicle license plates. There were not too many cars around, and a lot of people used bicycles and mopeds, like my Dad and Uncle Finch respectively.

CHAPTER 4

|||||||||||||||||||||||||||||||||||||||||| ||||||||||||||

CHANGES

Now that Granny was gone, everybody was afraid to go into the house alone after school. They were afraid of "jumby"/ ghost especially Joan. I was the only one who was unafraid, and my brother Walton to some extent. Our house key was kept across the street with Goodie Nurse, and the others would send me to get it, to open the house, and to be the first one in.

Life was never the same again after Granny died. There were numerous adjustments and transitions made in addition we had to grow up quickly. I already knew how to cook, clean; wash and iron, as I had learned from observation of Granny, Mom, Aunty Martha, Fanny and neighbours, plus Granny taught me to do things.

My grandmother has raised a niece, who was a twin: Martha George from Seatons Village and they are all related to Luther George. Granny took Martha as a baby, raising her as her own daughter; and then, years later, the other twin, Mary, also came and lived with us. They were identical twins however, each of them had a quirk eye and only Mom could tell the difference between them after she discovered what it was and then pointed it out to Granny. One had the quirk eye on the left while the other twin had her quirk eye on the right. They were like our aunts and, up to now, some people think their children are my younger siblings. Even after our grandmother died, others were brought into our household and were raised with us.

I remember Aunt Martha and Mary used to go and "pick cotton" and they would get on the tractor which picked up the workers in front of Mr Gillard shop afterwards they drop them off at Ms Browne corner at the end of the day. Essie and I would run up the street to meet them in the afternoons when they came back home.

Mom's friend Carolie Estela "Fanny" James used to help out in our home with the cleaning and preparations for Granny to cook, and was there when Clayton got burnt as a child with hot water and helped out when he was taken to the hospital. Fanny was a small woman, very tiny; however she had the biggest voice ever and was very talkative. She was full of confidence, vivacious, energetic and attentive. She would cuss you out in a minute and was never shy to use some expletives when you provoked her or interfere with people she cared about like Mom and our family and Mrs. Gonsalves whom she would do anything for as well. She used to wash clothes and scale fish for us and clean them up really good, she was great at it. One of Fanny's daughters is named after my sister Joan and Mom is her Godmother. Fanny was a staple in our lives and Mom always sent something for her from overseas. When she saw me she would say "you likkle garl fo Ms Tully." She was priceless.

Everything in our home completely changed after Granny died. Mom cried a lot, especially during worship on Sunday mornings and when she was by herself. Aunty Martha was the first to leave ... on a small boat then on to a bigger one that took her to England.

She migrated in 1957, leaving her two sons with us. Then my sister Joan and Aunty Martha's older son Essie went up to England to be with her. Her other son Danny followed, and then she had two more sons who were born in England.

... Mom was exceptional at her job at the Mill Reef Club, cleaning the guest rooms and setting up, serving, and breaking down in the dining room. She stayed on the hotel property all week and would come home on the weekends for her days off.

She was very much loved by the guests who came every year for vacation from the States. One of these visitors invited Mom to come to New York City to work for their family, and this she did for a few years. She would come back home to Antigua for a few months, then go back and forth as a domestic worker.

As children, we did miss Mom when she was away, but it was also good for us. We received a lot of letters with postal orders for our support and parcels with nice clothes that we loved and had enough to share with family members and neighbours.

Mom then left the States and went over to Canada, where, again, she worked with a family caring for their children in Rosedale, Toronto, Ontario.

At that time our three oldest siblings had already migrated overseas. Mom's firstborn, Patrick, who sang on the choir at Pilgrim Holiness Church and was a dedicated Christian, had left to study the ministry and become a pastor. He was already in Canada, attending "Briercrest Bible Institute" in Caronport, Saskatchewan, Alberta.

He had a very close friend with him, also from the Pilgrim Holiness Church and choir: Denny Grant. They were the only two Blacks there. It was real culture shock for my oldest brother – especially the food he ate: potatoes every day in every imaginable form; and he was longing to be home to eat rice and all the other foods. He said the place was very cold, with nothing but snow and more snow, and they did not have much of a summer.

Pat was very bright growing up, I was told by Dad and many others, including my cousin Eustace "Pops" Gordon. He would miss school sometimes because he suffered from asthma, but he would catch up very quickly. Pat worked at Dews on Thames Street for some time and left from there to Canada in 1960. He was a very big help to Mom in supporting the rest of the family.

Meanwhile, Mom's second child, Lloy, had migrated to the Virgin Islands. Lloy was not very academic, and he learn the mechanic trade with our Uncle Ally Hamilton, Aunt Eunice husband and their son our cousin Huon, and adopted brother Kenneth Evanson, he learnt from some of the very best and he became very good at it.

Mom tells a story of Lloy coming last in his class at school. When she questioned him about it, telling him that it was not good enough and that he must do better, he told Mom that "Last ah place!"/coming "last" was a place.

He was about to get a licking from Mom, but Granny told her not to beat him. Well, she decided that Lloy was *her* child and she was going to beat him, and proceeded to do exactly that. However, Granny had a "cancup" (a drinking mug made from tin) in her hand and threw it at Mom, catching her on the right foot just above the ankle, and cut her. My mother never forgot it, and recounted the incident well, right into her nineties.

Another time Lloy did not want to eat what had been prepared for lunch. Mom told him if he did not eat it now he will eat it for dinner, because that was what God had provided. In the end, he had to eat it; no one had food to waste back then, or to deal with the likes and dislikes of children.

Lloy became a very excellent mechanic and was a transmission expert; he worked on some of the best named cars in Miami, where he lived for many years until his death three years ago. At one point, he came over to Canada and tried living there with us. He had a very good-paying job at a car dealership where he was praised for his work and very much liked. However, he hated the winter weather and said it was even worse than when he was in New York. So he packed up and went back to Miami. Then some years later he came back to Toronto a second time to live, and again could not handle the cold, therefore he went back to Miami.

(Antigua is part of the Leeward Islands in the Caribbean and was still a colony when my family was traveling; so we were British subjects and had British passports. The country achieved statehood in 1967 and full Independence on November 1, 1981, establishing Antigua and Barbuda as a nation.)

Joan had already relocated to London, England, leaving us, the three younger children in Antigua. The last time Mom left for New York to make a better life for us, she placed me – the youngest child and a girl – with a relative who lived far out on Fort Road. We were not too happy about this, having Mom leave again and our older siblings were already overseas and now we were getting separated. As a young Teenager I felt a little sad, scared and alone especially having to leave the comforts of my own home to go and live with relatives in another home and in a completely different area and neighbourhood. My siblings and I had to make certain adjustments. I missed seeing my Brothers everyday and being in our own home plus seeing my Dad often.

This was not a good time for me; I was sad and miserable because I did not get to see my friends either. I was overjoyed when I was able to go to the country during the summer, to stay with my cousins, the James family, in Pigotts, my Uncle Sammy and his wife, my Aunt Mary. I was now comfortable and a happy child again. My Aunt Mary was loving, kind, caring, patience, thoughtful and a Mother who took really good care of her family and me. She had a big heart, and although she was raising a big family including Grandchildren she still had room, love and kindness for me. After my time there Dad said that Mom wrote and decided that I could go back home with my Brothers to our family home on Dickenson Bay Street/Back Street where I remained until I travelled to Canada.

Mom had a valise that she kept her good stuff in and also a trunk with her table linen, cutlery, dishes, glasses etc which she instructed us to give to Aunt Mary which we did before I departed to Canada.

My brothers and I took care of ourselves and each other. They were always protective of me, always looked out for me. We all knew how to cook and fend for ourselves. However, I prepared most of our meals, cooking all kinds of food, and kept the house clean, and they kept the yard clean. We went to school in the morning and came home for lunch, then went back in the afternoon until classes were finished at the end of the day. Everyone, back then, walked to and from school....

Now, classes did not start until we had Assembly in the morning, singing and praying before we were dispersed to our various classes. The subjects I did were History, Geography, English, Algebra, Geometry, Arithmetic, Religious Knowledge and Science. If you had extracurricular activities, like typing and piano lessons, like I did on certain days, then you would go to those after school, again walking back and forth from your home.

We had bullying in school, too. I was bullied by bigger girls when I first went to high school: I had long hair and they used to pull it. I remember a girl from The Point called "Perdue," who always interfered with me and call me "bony" because I was very slim. My friend Cheryl Challenger was slim, too, and they would try to figure out which one of us was skinnier and called us names. After my brother Clayton dealt with her and the others, and showed me how to stand up to them, the bullying stopped.

High school was not free of charge. My parents had to pay my school fees every term and buy textbooks. They also had to purchase new uniforms for me: a new hat and ribbons, shoes and socks, the tie that matched the jumper and the long-sleeved blouse, plus the white dress uniform. Our schools in Antigua did not have lockers, canteens/lunch rooms, gym room, basketball courts or swimming pools; nor any guidance counselors or a nurse.

In order to take care of their children, some adults made a living as cooks, and some washed clothes for other people. There were no washing machines at the time. We washed clothes by hand in big tubs, and put the whites on the "stone heap" where the sun would bleach them (no liquid bleach). We would sprinkle them with water periodically, then give the whites another rinse – adding some "blue" to the water – and finally pin them on the line to dry.

The education of many accomplished professionals was paid for by single parents who made their living as "washers." We had such a person do our laundry when we were by ourselves.

Some parents were hucksters/vendors who plied their trade at the Market, selling their fruits, vegetables, provisions, fresh milk, etc. Others sold from trays laden with sweets, sugar cakes, fudge, popsicles, and much more.

Back then, families living in the countryside sent their children to high schools in St. John's because that was where all the secondary schools were. Therefore, they boarded their children with family members and relatives in town. Other students only ate lunch with relatives on a daily basis, and then went home after school in the afternoon. This is what my relatives – the James family from Pigotts and the Georges from Seatons – did.

When my cousin Yvonne "Ineta" James moved to town to live with her Granny in our area, it provided me with a big sister, who made me happy and I loved her. I could tell her things and we used to spend a lot of time together after school. I remember going with her to the Trades and Labour Union building where her boyfriend, Roy, worked, printing the *Workers Voice* newspaper.

On Sundays we went to church on Thames Street, in Mr. Thibou's building on the southwest side from Newgate Street, where the First Baptist Church was started by persons like my Aunt Jean. I used to play chords on the organ for the songs we sang. After school I took piano lessons with Dr. Rock on St. John's Street, I recall he used a ruler to hit you on your hand when you got a note wrong.

However, that, too, came to an end as my cousin left Antigua on my birthday – September 23 – for Canada, on one of the schemes Canada offered at that time. It was Prime Minister Lester B. Pearson who started the process of opening up Canada, but Mom was already there. I missed my cousin, but I soon joined her, along with Mom and Pat, in Canada. I was one of the bridesmaids at her wedding; and she and Roy have now been married for fifty-three years.

During our school days, among the three younger siblings, Walton was very bright in all his school work, especially English, and writing was effortless for him. He was always in a higher form/grade than Clayton, our older brother academics were not for him, but he was very skillful in other areas.

Clayton's talents were in sports. He excelled in football/soccer, cricket, high jump and track and field. He played very well for the community soccer team and earned certificates and trophies. He was sent to learn different trades with various tradesmen. He was also great at woodworking and taking cow horns and shaping them into different things house wares ornaments etc.

Mom's life purpose for all her children was to give us a good education and provide a better life for us and her generations to come; and she was very determined and purposeful about it. Her mother had always told her that she had to make life better.

It was her intention to have the three of us leave Antigua and migrate to Canada at the same time, but that did not work out for us. Mom was still a domestic and "living in" with the family she worked for, and she did not have a place for us to come to as yet. Dad, at that time, was unprepared to relinquish all his children totally; therefore, he never completed the affidavit with the notary public that would give Mom permission to have us all travel to Canada and live with her permanently.

In the meantime, we were all growing up and getting older. Soon, Walton took a job at a hotel and then left the island; but not without first leaving a part of himself behind, as his girlfriend was pregnant. Then I left Antigua that same year to be with Mom after not seeing her for almost two years, leaving Clayton, the oldest of the three, behind by himself. Lloy our older Brother went back home to Antigua then Clayton migrated to Miami with him.

We all ended up being upstanding citizens with decency, good professionals, skilled workers, lawyers, doctors, politicians, bankers, police commissioners, farmers, teachers, judges, law-enforcement officers, hoteliers, financial controllers, pilots, business people, nurses, mechanics, foremen, executive housekeepers, maintenance managers, hotel and general managers, office clerks, governors-general, prime ministers, playboy bunnies, carnival queens, actors, ministers, priests, bishops, musicians, builders, draftsmen, masons, IT experts, mothers, fathers, grand and great-grand parents – accomplished individuals and so much more.

These are the persons I know who grew up in my generation and were brought up just like I was, and I do not know any murderers, serial murderers, or mass murderers among them, which is a fact that Mom was always very proud of.

CHAPTER 5

||||||||||||||||||||||||||||||||||||||||||||||||||||||||||||||||||||

LIFE IN CANADA

Mom continued to work as a domestic for many years in order to support her family. Then she was employed by a company called Drug Trading —doing office work - filing, collating, taking stock, and handling mail for many years until she retired at age sixty-five.

My mother went back to school in Canada and studied many things, earning a high school diploma and certificates in millinery (she made nice hats); icing cakes; and making cushions. Some of these were hobbies and she would still do some sewing. Mom loved hats and always wore the most flamboyant ones to church, with the matching purse, shoes, scarves and, always, her gloves.

Back then we attended the Walmer Road Baptist Church and, yes, we were the only Black family there for many years until Mom brought in some other Black people. She was part of the Women's League for many years, and as a teenager I was part of the youth group.

CULTURE SHOCK

In 1962, when Mom first arrived in Canada, there were hardly any Black people. She longed to see them and yearned for her own food from back home. She told us that, during the summer months, her employers went to their cottage, somewhere close to the Lindsey and Peterborough area. Once for dinner, all that was available was corn on the cob and a tossed salad.

Mom said her stomach hurt – she was so hungry – and she could not sleep that night. She just wanted to be back in Antigua with her children, and to eat her rice and mutton; her sweet potatoes; her fungie, choba/eggplant and saltfish; her provisions and dumplings, etc. She said many nights she would cry herself to sleep for missing us and her foods, and for not seeing any other black people for weeks and months.

My brother Patrick eventually moved to Toronto and was then attending the University of Toronto. He also had a part-time job and rented a room on Euclid Avenue near Harbord Street, where he shared the bathroom and kitchen with the other renters in the house. When Mom was off work on the weekends, she would go and spend time with him; cook West Indian foods; and attend church on Sundays. My brother would bring home other students, some West Indian and others from India and Africa, and Mom would cook up food and feed everybody.

Mom started making some friends in Canada the first among them were Cynthia and Willie Blunt from Barbados. She took over Cynthia's job with the family she worked with, as Cynthia had sent for Willie her Fiancée from Barbados and they were married. Mom was in attendance at their wedding and they became very close over the years.

She had other friends from Antigua also like Donald Lewis and his family, Mr. Huggins and family his son Dennis was a friend of mine we all hang out together as Teenagers with Terry Lewis and others, and Isalyn and George Williams.

Mom loved shopping and we would go from one store to the next on Saturdays when she was off. There were major landmark buildings and stores back then, like Honest Ed's, Loblaws, and Cabbage Town/Kensington Market, where Mom would buy stuff they were not even accustomed to selling, they used to look at her like she was crazy – cow heel; tripe; cow tongue, head and heart; then pig feet and tails, etc. But West Indian people ate these things. We would shop in Sears, Eatons, Simpsons, Dominion, and Woolworths.

MY ARRIVAL IN CANADA AND CULTURE SHOCK

I travelled to Canada by myself one Sunday afternoon in August. It was my first time going on a plane, and I did not like it. We arrived around eight at night. I believe I cried halfway on the journey to Canada, feeling sad about leaving Antigua, but I was also happy because I was going to see my mom and my brother Pat. The stewardess checked on me often, and I got encouragement from the lady sitting next to me. After I arrived at the airport and went through immigration, I got my suitcase and went to the other side, looking for my mom and brother. I did not see either of them there, and I saw only white people everywhere.

I got some change for the pay phone and called the number for my Mom where she worked and lived and got no answer, I was now feeling uncomfortable and cold because the sweater Mom had sent me was thin and not warm. I then called the number Mom had sent me for my Brother, when someone answered I asked to speak to him and they went and got him. He was shocked to hear my voice telling him that I was at the airport, he said they had no idea I was coming that day. I explain to him that Dad and I sent a telegram to Mommy informing her.

Mom was away at the cottage with the family she worked with and never received the cable that we sent. My Brother came to the airport to get me and we went to his place a rooming house on Euclid Avenue. Then Mom came from the cottage the following day and got me.

I lived with my Mom and the family she worked with at St. Andrew's Gardens in Rosedale, and on weekends we would go to my brother's place. He gave Mom and I his bed, and he would put the blanket on the floor and sleep there. This was not too bad, because we were in a house, like we were accustomed to back home in Antigua.

We eventually got an apartment on Danforth Avenue close to Donlands right on the corner upstairs a furniture store and that was our home for years. This, too, was a big adjustment for us: upstairs-apartment living then to high-rise apartment living. I left from that apartment and went on my own.

I attended the Jarvis Collegiate Institute, located on Jarvis Street at the corner of Wellesley. I had to take a bus, then the subway, changing lines at Young and Bloor, to get to my school.

Black students, at the time, were noticeably absent from that school, and when I spoke I was laughed at, because I had "an accent" and sounded different to everyone else, even though I spoke proper English. It was really severe culture shock.

On a weekly basis I had gym classes, pool period, English, Math, History, Geography, Science, and French. Some classes were outside in a "portable," and I had to go outside the main building, in the cold, to get to them. We had lockers for our coats, books, purses, lunch, etc. We stayed at school all day and had lunch in the cafeteria; nothing at all like what I was accustomed to in Antigua. At first I hated it and longed for home: my Dad, relatives and friends, my school, seeing people that looked like me, the warmth and sunshine.

When it rained heavily back home, there were no school; or we just did not go to school. So, the first time I saw snow, it was wonderful. I even enjoyed putting on my coat, boots etc and going outside in it. The next morning there was too much of it; however, here was my mother waking me up to go to school. I was thinking I would get to stay home and read my books and watch TV. I was annoyed, angry, and upset at my Mom telling me "no staying home." I had to put on boots and go out in this stuff to school. Boy, did I have plenty to write home about to my Dad, family and friends!

But I soon adjusted to all of these differences, and my transformation within a few years had me becoming Canadian. At age sixteen, I got a part-time job at the Wellesley Hospital, which was not far from my school. I had other schoolmates who also worked there, and we met lots of other young people and made friends. I even got reacquainted with persons that I had known from our church and community back in Antigua. I went to my school Prom and was escorted by my friend Marcus "Teddy" Jeffers who was also from my home Country Antigua, and we both had a good time even though this was all new to us.

I recall Mom having this pain in her side and stomach and she got to the Doctor right in time because they sent her directly to the hospital and they gave her surgery, for a problem with her large intestine. She was hospitalized for almost two weeks before she was sent home to heal further before going back to work. It was very concerning for Pat and I our first experience with seeing Mom sick like that and having to deal with her being hospitalized. I was really frighten, after only being reunited with Mom and in Canada for about a year and a half, then seeing her sick and vulnerable, especially in the hospital, I had already experienced two of my Aunts in Antigua who come out of the hospital dead and I was extremely far from ready for that with my precious Mommy.

Mom used to say I was too vain and worldly therefore when I told her I wanted to model she wasn't shock and she said that I wanted to do big things, and I was hanging my hat high. My Brother Pat said I was ready to conquer the world. We had a family discussion and I was eventually successful in winning their support. Mom's Boss had a Sister who had a TV talk show at lunch time on CBC named "Posie's Corner" she was very supportive and got me into "Cinderella School of Modeling" which I attended for months and was the only black person there. They had no skin care or make for black skin, only for white skin, which after a while became very uncomfortable for me. After High school I went to New York City where I attended a Black modeling school and I really learnt a lot and had my portfolio produced. I had a part time job in a collection agency and lived on my own and had some good modeling jobs.

Posie had me as a guest twice on her talk show, the first black person to be on it and they were other guest in the discussion of how it was for Caribbean/ Island people integrating into the Canadian culture, the way of life and into the communities. Mom and Pat were nervous for me, but I did well, and they later told me they were proud of me because I answered my questions well and explained my way of life back in Antigua good and proper.

Our School Choir which I was a part of had to perform at another school one night and afterwards I was invited out to join my school mates to go to a nearby Restaurant for something to eat, which was usually a burger and fries and either a coke, milkshake or a root beer. We were all walking to the Restaurant and I was the only black person as usual and then I suddenly realize that I see this figure coming towards us on the side walk and it was my Mother coming to get me, Oh NO! Is what I first felt. I had to leave with my Mom; we took the bus and subway home. No one else's parents came to get them, only my Mother. I was mortified; embarrassed and super upset with my Mom; I hated her in that moment. It did not matter how embarrassed I felt and expressed it to Mommy, she didn't care; she was taking care of her Daughter and being a responsible single parent.

Mom gave me a curfew to return home when I went out with my friends on the weekends. Because, for her, it did not matter if I got enough sleep or not. On a Sunday morning, I was getting up to go to church with her, never mind my age; and if she had to throw water in my face to wake me up, she was getting me up for church. My cousin Mel likes to remind me of one Sunday morning Mom woke us up to go to church and she said "I don't care all the funky broad off you did last night you getting up to go to church" the dance then was the "Funky chicken."

I was now going on eighteen years old and felt I should be able to stay out later than my curfew. So, one time when Mom was verbally disciplining me, I became mouthy and defiant. I told her that this is Canada, not Antigua, and I was past sixteen years old and could stay out as late as I wanted to, etc.

I was a size three or four and weighed less than a hundred pounds. But my Antiguan mother gave me a slap that knocked me to the floor. Then Mom sat on me and read me the riot act, as she continued to slap me on the head, face, leg, arm, and wherever – telling me something with each blow, that I was "not a big woman, she's the only woman here, she's the one that pays rent here.

She reminded me that she was the mother and I was the child; that I lived in her house, where she pays the rent, not me; and that two women could not live in the same house, and cockroach in fowl coop, etc. Patrick came home just in time to take her off of me and beg for me.

I never disrespected my mother since, and she lived to be almost ninety-three years old in my home with me. I learned my lesson very well. West Indian/Caribbean parents are loving people, but they are focused on raising their children right and administering discipline.

When I left the comfort of my mother's home, it was after attaining the milestone age of twenty-one, after returning to Toronto from NYC when Mom gave me a 21st Bornday/Birthday party. At the point of leaving home Mom cried and gave me a Bible to take with me. She also admonished me about doing the right things and trusting and believing in God in the way she had brought me up.

Mom and Pat were always helping others relatives to come to Canada. One cousin who received such assistance was the daughter of the relatives I stayed with when Mom left. In those days you had to have a certain amount of money to show Immigration; and after she arrived and was living with us,

Mom had some money saved in the bank which she withdrew and loaned to our cousin to help her secure her landed status. Afterward our cousin would not pay back the money.

Mom had to get the cashed cheque from the bank, with our cousin's signature on the back of it, and take her to court to get back her money. I remember how hurt and upset Mom was. Eventually, she and Pat had to tell the judge that Mom did not "give" her the money, as our cousin was claiming, nor did Mom owe her any money for repayment.

Mom further explained to the judge that she still had one child back home in Antigua to support, and she needed to get him out of there with that same money. The judge ruled in Mom's favour because of the evidence and our cousin had to pay back the money, plus costs, on a monthly basis. Mom spoke to Pat and I of lessons her Mother taught her "Not to borrow and not to lend, cause it mash up friendship/relationship," and she will not do that again.

It was very important to Mom that I got to Canada when I did because of Immigration laws which stipulated after age sixteen it was very difficult if not impossible for parents to get their children to come up. Mom and Dad were never divorced and she needed permission for us to live in Canada, therefore Dad had to give her permission especially for me, his child to be here permanently. He had to see a Lawyer and get an Affidavit giving Mom the legal right to have me in Canada with her permanently.

We had a lot of other family members who also came to Canada, especially when it "opened up." My cousin Ineta was one of the first relatives in Canada after Mom arrived. Then Pam/Yvonne Ineta's younger sister came up and attended university. Also Isalyn and George Williams and their daughter Denise and then they had Daryl, and then Sonia/Phyll her niece came up later on. Then my cousin Esther Bird came up around the same time. I was very happy when my Cousin Mel came to Canada. Finally, I had someone who was my age to hang out with, and we were always very close, like sisters, and did fun things together.

Mom and I went to New York in 1967, my first trip there. Mom and I were very excited to be going, especially to see my brother Walton/Muhammad. I saw my adopted brother Kenneth, and Aunt Jean, and other relatives and friends. I then started going to New York City every summer to spend time with my brother and his family; my sister-in-law and my niece Yolanda; my uncle Ken Tully and his family, Aunt Vera and my Cousins Favell, Yolette, Marlon and Natalie; and lots of other family members, which I enjoyed spending time with. My brothers took me to see all the sites in NY that first year. My brother Walton/Muhammad took me to the Apollo Theater in Manhattan for the first time and I remember we looked really good I was wearing a green and white polka dot chiffon dress that Mom had bought me and she was happy I looked great in it. We took a photo which I then sent back home to Antigua to our Dad and he treasured that photo forever.

When I went over to NY my Brother Walton/Muhammad used to take me out with him and his wife we went to the Apollo Theater and we went to clubs and restaurants and had wonderful times.

A few years later in NY I reconnected with my best friend, Valerie Harris, who had migrated from Antigua and was now living in the Bronx, right around the corner from my relatives, the Evansons' Aunt Jean, her brother and his wife and children, Kenneth, and my Niece Yolanda. It was a great reunion for us and gave me more reasons to visit more often.

As teenagers in Canada, we went to social gatherings in the late sixties. On Thursday nights, we went to Hi C on Bathurst Street in a church basement. On Tuesdays, we went to St. Christopher House, a community centre on Bathurst and Dundas Streets, and on Sunday afternoons, we went to Wiff Club, which was upstairs in a building on Brunswick and College Streets.

International basic human right was a very big issue, and the Black Power movement was real and alive. It expanded the collective consciousness, and it was formidable in its deliverance from ignorance. It instilled self-love and a great pride within black communities. The first march was established in May 1968 on the holiday weekend. On African Liberation Day, we marched from "Third World Books and Crafts Store" on Bathurst Street and it culminated at Christy Pitts Park. Many of us attended meetings to plan the march. My mom and my brother Pat met me on the road, and we marched together.

We went to Clubs as we got older such as "Le Coq d'Or" on Young Street and "Club Jamaica" which was owned by Fitz Riley and we enjoyed a lot of entertainment and all the music of Motown. There were acts such as Solomon Burke, Sam and Dave, The Cougers, Bob and Wisdom and The Fabulous Flames at Club Jamaica. They had talent shows and I used to win the dancing competitions. We went to Club Blue Note, Brunswick House, and Darcy's and of course the Yorkville Music scene.

All was well with Mom as long as I got home before curfew time. She made sure she knew all my friends and had their parent's phone numbers. I had a few friends and they were from all walks of life, Caribbean, Americans like my first friends ever Rosa and Linda Jones who came from Detroit, Canadians black and white. My other close friends were Liz Philbert and Jennifer Monteith. Mom did allow some of my friends to sleep over and I could sleep over at their homes.

I was out with my friend Charlotte one Saturday night and it was pass both our curfew, she kept saying don't worry I will think of something and she made up this big lie that the train had stopped running because of problems making us late getting home. My Mom was not accepting that she called Charlotte's Mom and sure enough we both told the same story, which was not good enough for my Mom she called TTC, public transport to confirm our story and we were busted and we both got grounded.

CHAPTER 6

||||||||||||||||||||||||||||||||||||||||||||||| |||||||||||||||||

FAMILY LIFE

Mom took over from her mother and has been adopting others into our family since back in Antigua. She once told me that she wanted to have a dozen children and she was blessed with six. Adopting persons into the family became very prominent here in Canada, where Mom adopted about a dozen persons from all over the Caribbean, India and Africa.

Mom became **"Mom"** to most persons and she liked that, from Pat's friends to my school friends; very few called her Mrs. Tully. The Children she took care of called her Veronica and the two youngest ones called her "Ra-na-na" because they could not say Veronica. She remained Mom until her passing.

One of her first adoptees was a young man from Jamaica, Michael Fisher, whom she met on the subway while traveling on the train, she saw him and was happy to see someone who looked like her and started up a conversation with him. Mom loved people and would talk with everybody, so she invited him to her church and to our home for dinner. Then when he brought up one of his sisters, Una Fisher, she, too, was immediately adopted by Mom. The relationship was so close that Mom would make both of us the same style dresses in different colours. Una eventually married Wakefield Simon and Mom was very supportive and involved in the wedding arrangements.

Mom had some very good friends back in Antigua – the Leblancs from St. Johnstons Village. They were a large family and she was close with all of them, from their parents down, especially Winnifred. While away, Mom and Brother Pat would assist them financially with the education of the grandchildren. One of the youngsters, Rudolph Davis, eventually travelled to Canada to attend university and lived with Mom and Pat.

He was present for many family situations and events and also his 21st birthday. I gave him a surprise celebration at my home, and he was quite shocked. We even invited a friend of his who had to fly there to surprise him. Rudolph is presently a very prominent citizen in Antigua and Barbuda and the Principal of the St. Joseph's Academy School. He is a multitalented individual with the voice of a nightingale; he sings on the National Choir and trains his school choirs and many others for different competitions and to perform for the National festivals of Carnival and the Independence celebrations. He is a great national of Antigua and Barbuda, and definitely one of Mom's special adoptees.

Mom's first adopted daughter would have been my best friend from childhood days, Valerie Harris, and her entire family – siblings; her husband, Conrad Pole; and her daughter, Candice Love, who is my goddaughter. And my other best friend Millicent "Sissy" McKinnon and her brothers Charles "Buntin" and George "Boogie."

At holiday times, Easter, Christmas, long weekends, Mom's home was full of all the people she had adopted, and she would cook up a storm and feed everybody. She would invite persons from her workplace if they did not have family in Canada, since she did not want them to be alone for the holidays.

Mom would host up to a dozen plus persons in addition to us for dinner and her food was very good, with the best black cake, bread pudding, and apple pies with ice cream for dessert. She always had gifts for everybody, especially the grandchildren, including the adopted ones.

Mom was an Entrepreneur for Christmas and other occasions she sold "black cakes," hats, and cushions that she made; and this was her income supplement, her extra holiday money especially for the Christmas season for her purchasing of cooking items and gifts. I was the marketing person, supplying most of the customers through my workmates and friends, and did most of the deliveries. In addition she had a few of her co-workers and church people as customers.

Mom had a ritual that she developed on Saturdays: She would only cook fungie and choba/eggplant and saltfish, with sweet potatoes and plantain on the side, and she would cook enough to feed herself on Mondays. Sometimes, she had so many families and friends coming by on a Saturday to feast on this dish that none would be left for her on Monday; but she did not mind giving to whoever came by.

I remember my Cousin Joe Reid, who was the president of the Antigua and Barbuda Association in the late sixties and early seventies, would come by after his Saturday meetings to eat Mom's food, and sometimes he might bring someone else with him.

My Mom just loved to cook and feed people and you had to eat off all that you were offered. She would always find something to cook white rice and a can of hereford corn beef and fry it with onions, tomatoes, thyme, green peppers and whatever else she had, then open a can of green beans or corn and put with it if she had. If she only had eggs it was an omelet or a can of sardines or salmon prepared in the same manner as the corn beef, and you had a full and balanced meal. She was very creative in her cooking. You could never be hungry in her home.

Mom was a very good cook and prepared the best meals, rice and peas, roast, beef, pork, chicken, Antigua season rice with pig tails or pig mouth and salt beef, chicken and beef etc; pepper pot and fungi; best Johnny cakes/fry dumplings they melted in your mouth, souse, macaroni and cheese, potato salads and on Good Friday it was always ducana with eggplant and saltfish. Her scallop potatoes and shepherd's pie was like her cakes and bread pudding, to die for.

The children she cared for also loved her cooking; they thought she was the best at it. She made them rice dishes and got them to eat it and the best hamburger because she would always season the meat before then grilled it or frying it just right.

In Antigua I recall her making over a hundred Johnny cakes/fry dumpling in her eighties that was requested of her for a funeral repast which she did not even get to attend after the funeral.

With Mom, you must have dessert after your meals and she was not eating her meals without her desserts she always left room for it, even a candy "sweetie" as she called it. Her favourite dessert was hot apple pie and ice cream, and her favourite candy was Werther's original which she always kept with other candies in a glass container on her coffee table and offered them to everyone that visited.

Canada celebrated one hundred years of Independence in 1967, and I went to Expo 67 in Montreal, on a field trip with my school. We stayed for about a week, and one of the oldest and best steel band orchestras from Antigua, "Hells Gate Steel Band," was there. I saw them perform and it was so exciting for me since I remembered some of the players because we were from the same village back home.

Hell's Gate Steel Band is the world's oldest, continuously operating steel orchestra. It's been around since 1946 and was the first steel band to ever do a recording. The band members make, tune, develop and produce their own pans and they have won the most awards and competitions during the Carnival celebrations and to date they are over seven decades old. Some of the pioneers were Eugene Weston, Eustace "Manning" Henry, George Williams, George "Nugget" Joseph, Walter "Motto" Bloodman and Bruce "Fundoo" Bloodman.

After performing in Montreal, they came over to Toronto and we had the opportunity to host them and Mom cooked up a storm and had them come over and fed them.

My Brother Patrick was one of the members who helped to create and execute the very first Caribana in Toronto Ontario it was the West Indians' community contribution to the occasion of Canada's 100 Birthday, Canadian Confederation Anniversary celebrations in 1967; Pat worked along with lawyer Charles Roach and others in the committee responsible in organizing and executing this Carnival. It was the first time I ever played Mas' in my life, and I was very happy that my brother persuaded Mom to allow me to take part. He also played Mas' that year as a Mountie Police. I played mas with Whitfield Belasco Band with some friends and other relatives.

Since then, I have been playing Mas' for many years – including as Queen of the Band and as an individual – and I would carry my banner proclaiming Antigua and Barbuda "The Heart of the Caribbean" which I sponsored myself.

My brother Walton, who lived in New York, migrated to Canada in the early seventies and Pat migrated to England for a few years. Mom and Walt then moved to a high-rise apartment on Victoria Park and Danforth Avenue. Mom no longer worked as a domestic and was now employed at Drug Trading Company in downtown Toronto.

Mom was always supportive and encouraging when you wanted to try something new and participate in community functions which she demonstrated with me all the time and when I entered the first "Miss Black Ontario Pageant" there was many contestants. It started out with one hundred and fifty of us vying for the title and about twenty of us on the night of the competition with five segments – introduction, swim wear, talent, evening wear and interview. I was sponsored by "Cute Toys" the first business, owned by a white couple to provide black dolls for purchase in Toronto for our black communities. Mom was involved in my evening wear assisting me in the colour, material and style selection in addition to my African dashiki for my talent segment of a black content skit, poem and sketch which I wrote and performed. I made it to the top ten and then sixth. My Sister Valerie came over from New York City for the weekend to give me support.

***

I sponsored Dad and brought him to Canada right after his sixtieth birthday in 1976. He lived with me, in my apartment, in an area called Cabbage Town; my building was on Parliament and Howard. I had some relatives and very close friends also living in the area. My cousin Dorothy Scholar, who was Dad's niece, and her young daughter, Stacey, lived nearby, and both Dorothy and I worked a night shift. I would also work at other jobs during the day, so Dad became the babysitter for Stacey and for a friend who sometimes brought her son to my home, too. It was not a paying job for him; he did it out of love.

I thought Dad would experience a hard time adjusting to living in Canada, after leaving his relatives and friends and, in general, his own life style in Antigua. He did not drink alcohol, except for some wine or champagne if there was a special occasion; but he never gave up smoking his cigarettes. That was fine with me, because I too was smoking at that time.

Dad liked it here and adjusted nicely in his own time. Being with the family made him happy, but he did admit he was missing Cricket, with the West Indies team batting and Viv Richards hitting sixes and making century after century. In the Cricket World Antigua and Barbuda Sir Isaac Vivian Alexander Richards KNH, OBE is King. He is one of the greatest batsmen of all time, known as "The Master Blaster" and Dad's most favourite to watch play whom he missed. However, he would get letters with all the news from his friend Mr. Michael and sometimes he would telephone him and he would catch up on all the news and happenings.

Canada was now our adopted country of choice providing and affording us an education, a living, and a home. In 1970, Mom, Brother Pat and I had become very proud citizens of Canada, the best country in the world, with one of the highest and best education and healthcare systems; it was a young nation and still a part of the Commonwealth.

We were all very happy that Mom had made that decision to leave New York and come over to Canada, making it her home and the home of the rest of the family and her generations to come.

Mom always longed for, and wanted to have, all her children around her. So Brother Pat and I organized a family reunion in 1977. My sister Joan and her son Eon, who was a boy at the time and Pat, came over from England, and my brothers Lloy and Clayton came over from Miami and Dad was already here from Antigua.

Both Mom and Dad were very happy to have the family all together again, and it truly meant the world to Mom to have her desire, the longing for her family, materialize. We had the best time together, worshipping, enjoying family dinners, going to a church that was similar to the one we grew up in back home in Antigua, with the very same pastor, Ira Taylor, being the minister.

For the few weeks we were all together, we talked a lot, laughed, and enjoyed dancing to the album Tony brought, *Family Reunion* by the original O'Jays. We experienced many adventures and went sightseeing at all the tourist sites in Toronto. Everyone loved Thousand Islands and Niagara Falls, and I recall Dad shedding a few tears at the falls. He was overjoyed to be there, and said it looked just like the postcards I had sent him. He said he was happy he had lived to see this wonder and thanked me for making it happen.

Mom, too, was happy, creating new memories with her family as we engaged in various activities together: going out to dinner, ordering in, and preparing Antiguan meals and great desserts, playing games as we did back home when we were much younger like snake and ladder and monopoly etc. My siblings then went back to their respective homes.

I used to work a few jobs modeling and then office work, through a temp service "Office Overload" then part time at Canada Post on the afternoon shift for two years; this is where I met Maggie Daniel-Manson who was working two jobs also. At age twenty six with hard work and help from God, I purchased a three bedroom condominium, and Dad and I soon moved in. We lived in Don Mills on York Mills Road, close to the 401 Highway. I was now working full time at Canada Post and transferred to the day shift on wickets working in the area of the philatelic stamps, parcels, etc.

Dad went to New York a few times and visited with his brother Ken and his family, also his niece, Gloria Gordon-Lewis, and took care of her daughter a few times. He spent time with his nephew, Victor Scholar, and Cousin Victor came over to Toronto and visited with us, when I travelled to Antigua for Carnival taking some friends with me, while he kept Dad's company.

Dad wanted to work and got himself a job at the University of Toronto, located in downtown Toronto. He worked in the kitchen area which provided for the cafeteria. Dad would take the bus and subway back and forth, and when it was really cold I would pick him up after his shift and Mommy after work.

Dad was a small-bodied man, and during the winter, that wind factor felt like it was going to pick him up and take him away he told me and that he needed two weights, one for each hand, to keep him down, balanced and protect him from the wind, and we would laugh about it.

Dad had the pleasure and joy of knowing six of his grandchildren, and spent time with them. He held some as babies to toddlers and through grade school, starting with Kenneth in Antigua; Eon, the first grandchild; Yolanda, Addie, Akil, and Yusuf – five children of Walton aka Muhammad Hadi Abdullah, who, at age twenty-one, was married with two children and was working hard and taking care of his family while living in New York.

Dad was never a sick person; however, after he first arrived, he had surgery on his prostate – for what he called "stoppage of water." All went well and he was as good as new. One Saturday I left him and went to get my hair done and then to run some errands; and while Dad was taking a shower, he fell in the bath tub and broke a few ribs. Back then there were no cell phones to keep in touch. Dad called Walton/Muhammad, who came to his rescue and got him to the hospital.

The Plaster could not be applied on his ribs; therefore, the hospital bandaged him up with tape, to which he ended up being allergic, as it continually itched and took off his skin. I had to take him back the following Monday morning to get it all sorted and replaced. That was the extent of any serious medical issues with Dad until a few years later, when I observed his breathing began to be very heavy, short, and laboured.

I took Dad to the doctor and then to a specialist who ran different tests. At first he said Dad might have emphysema; but after further examination and testing Dad was diagnosed with lung cancer. He was encouraged by the doctor to have surgery and, since he was told that he could live with one lung, Dad went along and had it. After the surgery, there were treatments of cobalt/radiation every week, back and forth, at the Wellesley Hospital.

During his sickness he had some visits from family and friends and my siblings and all the family in New York would call often to check on him. His friend Mr. Burns visited and also his friend Novel H Richards Sr. who at the time was the High Commissioner for Antigua and Barbuda.

Dad's condition did not improve; it worsened as he got weaker with the spread of the cancer, until he died on April 26, 1981.

It was definitely well with his soul. Prior to Dad's passing at the hospital, he asked for Mom, and she was the last person he saw before taking his final breath seven minutes later.

It was my first experience arranging a funeral, and our family's first death experience in Canada. It was painful losing Dad, who died twelve days before his sixty-fifth birthday. But he got a good send-off, with Lloy and Clayton coming in from Miami and other relatives from New York, including Dad's brother Ken and his entire family. After the burial everyone came back to our home for a repast.

Now that Dad had passed, I had a big three-bedroom condominium to myself; therefore, I asked Mom and Brother Pat to move in with me, which they did. I left wickets and went back to working in the plant on the night shift at Canada Post. After about a year, Pat decided to complete medical school and wanted to move back to Antigua. He then left Canada for a medical school in Santo Domingo, intending to return to Canada in three years, and then go back to Antigua to give service.

Mom and Pat were always very close; they had a special bond. The two of them would discuss matters and make decisions about our family and our lives, and determine how and when we should and would do things. He helped Mom raise the rest of us as a big brother, working and helping out the household with financial and emotional support, since we were children back in Antigua.

He had made several moves and had to make many adjustments. He moved from Antigua to Saskatoon and then to Toronto. He also moved to England and lived there for two years, teaching high school and counseling families and youth, and then he returned to Canada.

Brother Pat had several degrees and certificates in various disciplines, including a BSc. in science, Ph.D in computer science, teaching, languages – Spanish and French, accounting, counseling and law; including working as a nurse at Roncesvalles Hospital for a few years.

Prior to him leaving Canada, he had started a Church of Spirituality with some associates. They based their beliefs on the meaning of life, connecting with others, living in peace and with a purpose, the individual energy of a person, and following Christ's principles. When they opened their doors for the first service, Mom, Muhammad and I attended, giving him our support. I went back a few times by myself and liked it, and felt connected to them.

December 5, 1982 was a Sunday, and after Mom and I had dinner and relaxed a bit, we discussed the things we were going to get done that week, as Brother Pat had requested in the last letter we had just received. I then went to lie down and get some rest before going to work at 11 pm.

I had a dream during my sleep, and saw Pat lying on a slab; he was pointing at me and trying to say something to me. I got up and started preparing myself for work. The phone rang, and when I picked up, it was my friend Maggie, and I remember sharing my weird dream with her. Mom was now already in her room and in bed. I put the dream down to getting the things done for Pat, as requested.

My shift ended at 7am, and I would usually go right home. However, that morning I had made arrangements to see a friend, Keith Sheppard, whom we called "Fifty." I then went home, and by that time Mom would have already been at work downtown. There was a note stuck in my door that said "I am a priest and I need to speak with you urgently. Please call this number. It is imperative."

I called the number but he would not tell me what he needed. Instead, he said he would come back and talk with me. I let him in the door and he announced that he had sad news: He reported to me that my brother Patrick had died the night before in the Dominica Republic. Well, I almost had a heart attack! I screamed, "No no no! It cannot be! They probably have the wrong person."

After the priest left, a police officer arrived bearing the same news. I then got a phone call from the Parliament building in Ottawa, giving me the news and confirming Pat's passport number.

After I was able to calm myself and think, I realized I now had to go and get Mom from her job. I picked up the telephone and called Walton/Muhammad, who lived not too far away, and he said he would be right there and drove over. We hugged and cried and then decided we would go get Mom; he did the driving. When we arrived at Mom's job, she was on lunch and had left the building for an errand. We were both terrified about how we would break the news to her. It was the worst thing we both ever had to do.

Mom finally got back from her lunch break and there we were. Instinctively, she knew something was not right. She said she had just come from the bank, where she had wired some money to Pat as he had requested. We tried to get her to sit down, but she would not. She asked what had happened and, after a while, Muhammad said, "Mom we have bad news. We got a report that Pat died."

She looked directly at me and asked, "Which Pat? Your Pat?" You see, I was dating a man called Patrick, and he was in Trinidad, his birth country, at the time. Muhammad and I, at the same moment, told her, "No, Mom. Our Pat." She immediately became limp and was about to fall when we held onto her. We left her work place and went home. I contacted our family doctor who came by in the evening and gave us a prescription for a sedative for her.

This was shocking news for our family; he was still young only forty four years old. I called my other three siblings and told them the bad news – Joan and other relatives in England, Lloy and Clayton in Miami, and all our family here in Canada, the States and in Antigua.

Consulting with Mom, I organized Pat's funeral and made all the pertinent arrangements. I had his body shipped back to us in Canada and had a funeral home collect and prepare it for burial. We all went to the funeral home after his body arrived, Mom and four of her children, since Joan did not make it over.

All the way to the funeral home, I was hoping that when we got there it would not be Pat, and all of it would just be a mistake, a dream that I would wake up from – not even knowing, at the time, that we were all having the same thoughts, especially Mom.

On seeing his body we were all disillusioned at first, because it *was* him; we were then shocked, angry, beside ourselves, and screaming, hollering, groaning, moaning and crying, this was now a reality. Then I had to put all emotions aside and hold up Mom. My brothers helped and held on to her, as we surrounded her and tried to comfort her.

Family members and relatives came in from Montreal and New York to lend support and to attend Pat's funeral at the church he had started. At one moment during the service, Mom got up and just laid the top portion of her body on his casket, crying. All I could do at the time was to go up to her and just hold her, until I succeeded in getting her to come back and sit down.

The burial was just as devastating, as Mom was just limp and wanted to go down in the hole, too. We finally made it through and returned to our home for a repast with the family and close friends.

Everyone now went back to their respective homes and we were left alone to cope the very best way we could. Now, trying to return to normalcy is not really possible after a death in a family like ours, for life is never, ever, the same.

I went back to work on the night shift but could not leave Mom alone all night by herself. So I took her to Olive, Mom's adopted daughter, with whom she would spend the night and leave for work in the morning, then I would pick her up from work at the end of the day and repeat this routine until the weekend when I was off. This went on for a few months before Mom felt comfortable staying by herself. I again changed my shift and went back out on the wickets to work on the day shift.

***

Mom and I loved to dress up and go out. I took Mom out with my friends and relatives to the theater, many restaurants, and shows. We went to the "Imperial Room" at the Royal York Hotel very often, and we saw many celebrities – including Pearl Bailey, who acknowledged us in the audience, talked with us, and then sent a bottle of champagne to our table. We saw Tina Turner when she released her hit album at that location, and we saw Ella Fitzgerald, who gave mom her autograph.

On one occasion I booked dinner for us – Una Hayles, Beryl, Norma, Betty, Mom and I – and then the theatre, at another location, to see a play called "Let my people come." It was a very unusual and interesting night, starting at the restaurant. Two gentlemen sitting at the next table noticed us and decided to engage me in conversation, and we just had a great time through the meal. One of them paid for Mom's and my dinner and then decided to join us at the theatre if they could get in without reservations.

We got to the theatre, and we all got in and were seated. Then, as the play began, the actors came onstage naked. We were surprised, as it was not what we expected, and one woman started to act like a prude. I immediately apologized to my mother and asked if she wanted to leave. My mother's response was, "No, Picknee. Me see naked people before; they have the same things we have. And we already here."

Everybody just exhaled, laughed, then complimented her, telling her that she was the greatest and had the right attitude, and gave her kisses. We all stayed and enjoyed the production. It was one of our most memorable outings and we often spoke and laughed about it.

Mom continued to work and retired at age 65 and I also retired from the Canada Post and pursued other avenues of career and work. We applied for a senior's apartment for Mom, which we got in a very nice building on Sheppard Avenue, right across from Agincourt Mall, where Mom resided for many years.

The six gifts of life Mom delivered were her blessings and she ensured their education and that they had the opportunities overseas for a better life for themselves and her future generations. She was very proud of all of Brother Pat's accomplishments and the degrees and certifications he pursued, as he was very determined to achieve. I recall one time he had problems getting a job because they said he was "over-qualified."

Mom's apartment wall had his degrees and certifications all lined up, at least nine of them, and this was after his passing. When he was alive he did not display them; therefore Mom was making up for that, because she was still proud of him.

CHAPTER 7

||||||||||||||||||||||||||||||||||||||||||||||||||| |||||||||||||||

TRAVEL AND ADVENTURE

After retiring from Canada Post, I first rented out my condominium and then I took Mom to London, England, where we teamed up with my childhood friend and her mother, who had traveled from Antigua to England. My friend had brought her mom there to celebrate her 50th birthday and all four of us went on a European tour.

We crossed The Channel and then embarked on our two-week tour. We first visited Belgium, then Paris, where we went to the Eiffel Tower and The Louvre. Mom was amazed that she was actually in these places, and she cried for joy and thanked me. We went to Luxembourg. In Venice we rode in a gondola on the canals. We visited Austria and the Black Forest (the mountainous region of Germany) and rode in the cars on the zipline. In Switzerland we saw cows wearing cowbells, and we traveled to Liechtenstein. We saw numerous beautiful hotels, churches, magnificent and historic edifices.

We spent six weeks in London with Aunt Martha and her family and visited Eon, the first grandson. We witnessed the Changing of the Guard at Buckingham Palace and visited London Bridge and the Crown Jewels, Madame Tussaud's, St. Paul's Cathedral, the Tower of London, and many other places.

I celebrated my birthday there in September, as did Aunt Martha's son, Fitzroy, and my friend's Mom, just days apart. My aunt and her husband Kenneth gave us a wonderful birthday party that was special and unforgettable.

It was a great experience for us, being in England and seeing the family after so many years – especially my cousin Essie, and Danny – and meeting

Aunt Martha's other children whom we had not met before and other family members who were born there.

On returning to Canada, Mom went back to night school and took some courses in icing cakes and cake decoration. She started doing some volunteer work at the North York General Hospital, which she took very seriously. It was a long way from where she lived, and it did not matter the weather: She was not going to a miss a single day of being present. Mom did this work for fifteen consecutive years and enjoyed it tremendously. After ten years the hospital recognized her at an official function at which time she received a certificate and a gift.

***

Mom's first great-grandchild, Kenneth's first child Omari was born on her bornday, and some others were born on the same dates as her children and grandchildren. She was present at the hospitals for most of her grandchildren's births, not only in Canada but also in the States.

She spent a great deal of time with her Grandchildren specifically the four youngest ones Akil, Yusuf, Safiyyah, and Imran all born in Canada. There are five of them, Adewale "Addie" Olusegun was the first born, however he was taken away from Canada overseas and we did not have any contact information for him. Mom purchased them very nice clothing, books and toys, no birthdays, holidays or special occasion was ever missed, they were all well provided. I recall them as babies we would babysit them and they would fall asleep on my chest on the couch we have numerous pictures of them growing up. Mom adored them and enjoyed shopping for them, especially those cute little dresses for Safiyyah. Sometimes I took them to Chuckie's or KFC for their Bornday celebrations with their friends and neighbours, they had fun and a great time. She also baby-sat for some of her great grand nieces and nephews to include Alliston and Nikaila Davis who also travelled with her to Antigua and back to Canada and Real Hamilton Romeo and Risa Hamilton Lightfoote when they came over to Canada during the summer months.

Mom had the opportunity of being involved in the life of her second grandchild Kenneth, born in Antigua where he was raised by his great-grandmother, great grand aunt and his grandfather on his Mother's side living with them since his birth. On our side of the family he had our Father and Uncles especially Uncle Theodore Finch whom he saw very often and his son Duncan had a son Peter, that lived right next door to Ken and they grew up together playing as children.

Mom would always send money to help out with Ken's support at holiday times in particular. I personally took an interest and ensured that on a monthly basis I would send remittances for his support. I visited him during Carnival times, taking him clothing, school supplies etc. I was trying to bring him to Canada when he was about ten years old, an adoption was required to make it possible however his Mother who lived in NYC was not ready to relinquish at that time. I eventually succeeded in bringing him up to Canada when he was still a Teenager and he lived with Mom and me. We tried our best to instill in him good values, principles and decency. I also booked him in a technical school to learn a trade.

Kenneth had also left a son in Antigua Omari Sr and before a year was up decided to return to Antigua to care for his child and girlfriend. Then after about a year and a half if that long, in Antigua he asked me to return to Canada. I then sponsored him with Immigration and he returned. He lived with me, and I registered him in George Brown College to learn "mechanic" and then he practiced and worked at "City Auto Electric" with Lascelles Carby.

Ken was very good at football since back in Antigua and he also played for the Toronto team "Simba" and sometimes we would go and watch him play. He would go out with my car on the weekends with his girlfriend and friends. I threw him a twenty first Bornday/Birthday party with his friends and family in attendance and Mom made him a great big cake iced with all the things he liked. And Yolanda came over to Canada a few times during the summer and spent the time with Mom and me and visited with her younger siblings.

Mom was a nurturing person and full of plenty faith. The worst winter months are in December to February, bitter, treacherous and dangerous weather and when things get planned they can be easily cancelled and postpone due to inclement weather and Mom's Bornday is in the heart of it. I recall organizing a dinner party at my home for her in celebration on the Sunday in 1987 where I invited some family and friends. I had everything prepared and did a lot of cooking, however Caribbean people are the first to cancel out at the very first sign of bad weather, that afternoon freezing rain started to come down and I left my home to go to Mom's home to pick her up to come back to my home. I did not get there I had a bad accident on highway 401 where two cars clip mine the second spinning me around where I collided head on with another vehicle.

I was unconscious but I remember briefly being in the ambulance and at the hospital. I was in and out of consciousness and I remember giving my name when asked then blank and then thinking if I was alive or dead, I didn't see Jesus or hell fire, somewhere along I just felt too much pain all over my body from my head and face down, then blank again for some time until I heard my Mother's voice praying and then telling me to "Louie wake up, wake up, wake up now" while holding my hand. Mom's prayers and faith pulled me threw and she wasn't about to bury another child. Sometime afterwards Ken showed up after not coming home the Saturday night and then my Brother when I was becoming more conscious. The hospital went through my purse, got my Identification and called Mom who therefore took a taxi to the hospital. My car was a complete write off but not me thank God. My seat belt secured me by saving me from going through the windscreen.

***

I sold my condo and went back to college and did courses in Hospitality Management; Hotel and Restaurant Operations; Food & Beverage Management; Management Skills; Front Office Management; National Sanitation Training; and Corporate Communication. Afterwards I worked at the Prince Hotel and also at Sutton Place Hotel for a few years, respectively. I then decided to move back to Antigua after being encouraged by Valerie and my partner, which I did in November of 1989.

I first worked with the Government in the Tourism Department with Yvonne Maginley and Edie Hill Thibou and in addition taught part time at the Hospitality Training Institute for many years, and then I worked as an Executive Housekeeper with Sandals Antigua for a number of years. I had Mom come down and visit with me once a year, during the winter months, especially in February for her birthday to get out of the cold and enjoy the warmth, sunshine and beaches then I would go up and visit with her during the summer months every year and sometimes more.

In February 1990 I had Mom come down for her Birthday and my Partner and I was to pick her up from the airport but we had an accident where he damaged his mouth and had to get stitches and I sustained a broken left arm in three places with a chip bone floating. Valerie had to collect Mom from the airport for me and tell her about the accident. As soon as Mom got to the house she was down on her knees praying I was told. At the Hospital the Doctor operated on my arm to reset it but two days later he had to reset it again without giving me any anesthetic, it was extremely painful, but Mom was there with me praying and giving support. My arm was still not fixed properly and I eventually had to go up to Canada to get it sorted out.

While in Canada Mom continued to support the Antigua and Barbuda Association functions Mother's day Brunch and the Independence Church service and carrying the Antigua flag she was very proud doing that. This was all possible with the help of some of my friends who would pick her up and take her back home Eric Delfish and the late Kenroy Stevens.

Some very kind friends Ernest and Veronica would pick her up on Sundays and took her to Church and back since they worshipped at the Walmer Road Baptist Church also and were regular visitors to our home and the dinner parties for all the occasions.

During that time, family members and friends would always check on Mom. I had three adopted sisters who would visit her regularly and take her out: Olive Isaacs, Maggie Daniel, and Una Hayles. Mom adopted Myrna Newman and her sister and even had the sister and her daughter live with her for a while. Family members would call frequently and speak with her including my Uncle Earl and Aunt Myrtle Tully who lives in NY and visited us in Canada and also about three times in Antigua, he always said that Mom was his favourite Sister in law and she shared the same sentiment for him.

Mom would always provide shelter for those in need. When I was a teenager, a friend of mine became pregnant and her parents put her out of their home. Her boyfriend was also from Antigua and was like a big brother or cousin to me; we were very close. When they called and told me she had been put out, I told my Mom. She said, "Tell her to come; she can stay here with us." And she did. This situation also happened with a relative of ours whom I love dearly, and she lived with us, also.

Mom loved and admired Nelson Mandela; Dr. Martin Luther King, Jr.; Oprah Winfrey, whose show she watched on a daily basis; Prime Minister Pierre Elliott Trudeau, Bishop Dr. Desmond Tutu; Michael Jackson; and Princess Diana. She would read magazines about them and put their pictures in albums and in her scrapbook. She got the opportunity to see Dr. Tutu when he visited Toronto. Mom didn't care how many people were going to see him; she got on the bus and subway and went by herself.

Mom had made some friends in her building and was soon feeding them her black cake, bread pudding, and West Indian food. And she got to know their children and grandchildren, too, and they hers. She would sometimes attend functions in the recreation room, and she would go on bus trips to The States and other places also other seniors' outings, which she enjoyed.

Mom would send the TV Ministries her money, Jimmy and Tammy and she would buy the books they were advertising. I told Mom to stop sending them her Pension money because they did not use it to help people in need; they lived lavishly and used it for their mansions, cars and planes. Mom said to me "that's on them, they have to answer for themselves and that don't have to do with me giving because I give to do good and help"

CHAPTER 8

||||||||||||||||||||||||||||||||||||||||||||||||||||||||||||||||

FAMILY CARE AND SUPPORT

Mom's fourth child, and one of her favourite children, was Clayton, whom we called "Tony." He lived in Miami. In 1994 he became ill and it took the doctors some time, with examinations and different tests, before they diagnosed him with lung cancer.

Mom, Muhammad, and I took turns visiting him and his family. I visited for a week, and then went over to Toronto to spend time with Mom before returning to Antigua. Afterwards, Mom spent two weeks with him and, on her return to Toronto; Muhammad went over and spent about a month, taking Tony for his treatments and doctors appointments.

I would call often to encourage him and to keep abreast of his condition. Clayton's situation deteriorated, and on his bornday/birthday, October 12 which made him forty eight years old I called him, but he was not coherent nor aware it was his bornday. I took a flight to Miami the next day and got the ambulance to take him to the hospital, where I remained with him until he passed.

The day before he died was a Saturday. He woke up, very conscious, and wanted to know why he was in the hospital and what was going on. He said he was fine, felt great, and nothing was wrong with him and he wanted to go home.

The mother of his children, Wendy, and his best friend, Jimmy, were both visiting at the time. I called Mom and had him speak with her and then with Muhammad. We talked and laughed and he spoke with his children, he had one boy and two girls: Corey, Chatoni and Chanta Tully.

This was amazing, and we could not figure out what was happening, either. This situation lasted for about an hour or more and then Clayton went right back into the same unconscious state as before, and was never conscious again. He died the following day. Again I had to be the bearer of bad news to Mom and the family.

Clayton was the athletic one in the family. Any sport, he was there and was good at it: cricket, track and field, high jump, and soccer. He loved all the contact sports in North America, and not only watched them on TV; he attended the games, as well, especially the play-offs. I recall him saying that he wished we had moved to North America when we were small children, because he would have been a football or soccer great, and Mom responding saying yes, she believed him.

Mom, Muhammad and my partner Terry traveled over from Toronto to Miami and we made funeral arrangements for him. Our sister Joan came from England for his funeral; they were always very close since we were children. Mom now had to bury another favourite child. She did better this time in dealing with it; however Joan was distraught, especially during the funeral service and the burial. Only Muhammad could handle and comfort her.

As we returned to his home from the funeral, my boss called and summoned me back to work at the hotel. I returned to Antigua the very next day, leaving my family and my partner in Miami: Mom, my two brothers, Lloy and Muhammad, and my Sister Joan and partner Terry. They spent another five days there and then went back over to Toronto and Joan went over with them and spent a week with Mom before returning to London England.

Losing Clayton was hard on everyone – his girlfriend; Corey, his fourteen-year-old son; and his two daughters – Chatoni, eight years old, and Chanta, who was six and a half. Mom was back in mourning, Lloy was not doing too well, Muhammad was not in a good place, either, nor was Joan or I.

We all tried to be supportive of each other, especially Mom. I made sure I checked on her more often by calling on the phone more frequently, and by sending her cards, letters and packages. I visited as often as I could and had Mom visit with me more often in Antigua.

One of the worst things for any mother is to bury any of her offspring; all parents would like to get old and have their children bury them. But Mom had now buried her husband and her two favourite children. I remember her saying it feels like somebody has pulled out your heart and your stomach from your body at the same time, and your head or anywhere else didn't feel right. She never imagined she would have to bury her son Pat and now her son Clayton. Her expectation would have been for them to bury her; however, as she opined, it was God's will.

Mom had to deal with many adversities and challenges in life. Mom was hypertensive; it started when she became pregnant with me, her last child, and it continued after my birth. When I was a child growing up, she used all the right bushes and herbs to control it. Then, later on in life, she was put on medication for her condition.

Mom learnt to cope and rely on her God for His grace, strength and comfort. She kept busy with her volunteer work at the hospital and her church groups, and with making her cakes, bread puddings, cushions, and hats.

CHAPTER 9

||||||||||||||||||||||||||||||||||||||||||||||||| |||||||||||||

MOM'S MIGRATION
BACK TO ANTIGUA

Over the years, Mom got up in age and was now in her late seventies, she was actually seventy nine years old. I ensured that I spoke with her a bare minimum of twice each week, but most times more, and I noticed that when we spoke she would repeat herself often. When I would say to her, "Mom, you said that already," she would reply, "I have to make sure you hear me and understand."

I believe this was the first sign that she was now in a bit of trouble and, in addition, she would tell me her blood pressure was high and did not seem to be going down. I would ask her why, whether she was worrying about something; if she was eating properly; and if she was taking her medication; and she would always say yes. I remember discussing it with Muhammad and he said she watches Oprah daily and when Oprah deals with certain issues she gets upset and cries along too so that could be a factor sending her pressure up.

It was during Fall/Autumn going into winter that I therefore decided to go up to Toronto to check on her. On my arrival I discovered she was not taking all of her medication, so I took her to the doctor and got that straightened out. But I realized she needed care, and I immediately packed her suitcase and brought her to Antigua. This was in November 1999.

At that time I was doing consultation and training, after establishing my business a few years prior "Tully's Hospitality Consultation and Training," working at Cross Roads Treatment Center, Jolly Harbour and other hotels a few days each week; while managing my partner's band.

My partner, Terry Lewis, award winning musician/bassist songwriter/producer and I founded a theatre group with some talented teenagers, "Corn Alley Performing Arts Group & Production," and we produced original plays, lyrics, and music and had performances a few times each year at the Cathedral Cultural Centre. In addition, we had a singing group of four very talented young ladies and we named them "4Tune." We had a production in December and took Mom and she really enjoyed it. The group also performed at Jumby Bay and Mom was in attendance. We had a good Christmas and then it was the New Year; and right around the corner, in February, was her eightieth bornday/birthday.

I organized a tent on my front lawn with all the trimmings to celebrate Mom's eightieth Bornday and invited our families, the Adams, Hamiltons, Gordons, Finches, James, adopted family, and friends, and she had a wonderful time, with relatives and church members making speeches and giving cheers. Terry and the lead singer from his band, "3D Hardway," Bruce Harris, performed a few songs for her. It was really memorable and made her happy. We had lots of food, drinks, and cake. Mom received bouquets of flowers and other gifts, including the pearls I bought her, and she was happy.

After that occasion, I ensured every bornday from then on was celebrated: having family and friends over or going to a restaurant or a hotel for dinner. I have taken her to St. Lucia and another time to Dominica, and a few times we had a luncheon for her at the Center after worship. She liked this and always looked forward to her bornday celebrations.

During the summer we went back up to Toronto, where I gave up her apartment, packed up some of her stuff, gave away all her winter clothes, dishes, hats, furniture, cushions, etc. I did ship a few pieces of her furniture down to Antigua. She was reluctant, at first, to be relocated to Antigua, because she loved Canada and wanted to keep her apartment and continue to live there. She did not want to give up her independence, which was understandable.

I explained to her that she would be better off with me in Antigua and related all the good things we would do. I told her she would be able to spend time with her siblings – Uncle Georgie, Aunt Martha and Uncle Kenneth, who had built a home and moved back from England, and her niece, Nola

Hamilton-Davis, who lived just down the street from me. These situations helped to make her feel more comfortable about the move. Most of her friends and the people she knew were already passed away either in Antigua or overseas which is something she mentioned. There were a few persons left whom she knew from her school days growing up whom she had relationships with Mrs. Anna Hurst, Mrs. Ruth Lewis, and Dame Gwendolyn Tonge whom she did visit with, time and again.

On our return back home, I hired someone to work with us for five days each week, while I was on my job, to care for Mom by ensuring she was fed properly, eating all the right foods; that all her medication and vitamins were taken in due time; and to keep the home clean and tidy.

I got a nice Guyanese lady named Maxine King, a mother of five children, four of whom were still back in Guyana. But it was not for long, as she soon brought them all here to Antigua – the youngest, her only daughter, being about four and a half years old upon her arrival.

Maxine was the perfect fit for us: Mom was happy with her, even though she gave her a little trouble now and then – to keep Maxine on her toes, she would say. Mom was never a complainer; she was easy to care for and had good conversations with everyone; and she could be very funny and entertaining and would keep you laughing.

CHAPTER 10

IIIIIIIIIIIIIIIIIIIIIIIIIIIIIIIIIIIIIIIIIIIIIIIIIIIIIIIIIIIIIIIII

LIFE IN ANTIGUA

One day each week Mom and Maxine would go to the senior citizen gathering that was headed by Mrs. Thibou and to all their outings. I had a taxi-driver "Wallace" pick them up at home and take them, and he would go back and collect them when they were ready to go home. Maxine liked this aspect of her responsibilities also and, by natural progression, soon became one of Mom's adopted daughters. Maxine was also very good with looking after family and friends when they visited with us from overseas and they also appreciated her.

Mom got to spend time with her brother; her niece Nola who visited often; and Aunt Martha, Kenneth, and her cousin Merle. I would take them to the beach and sometimes into town to get ice-cream, and hang out at Heritage Quay and Redcliffe Quay. At other times I would drop Mom off at Uncle Georgie and then go back for her later. At Christmas time I would take Mom, Nola and Aunt Martha driving in the country and everywhere for the "Lighting Competition." We enjoyed looking at the Christmas lights, the themes and creative work they had put into it.

We went to the beach a lot and had picnics, but, most times, just for a dip and to walk along the sand and then back into the water. Mom could swim and we all enjoyed seeing her do a little of that.

When Mom first arrived back home, she would go for walks every day in the neighbourhood and became familiar to everyone. She read her Bible first thing every morning, as she did her worship and prayers for years. She liked to sit on the back patio and eat the fruits from our trees: pawpaw, finger rose, guavas, cane, sugar-apples, soursop, pomegranate and mangoes. Mom would feed the mango skins to our dogs, which they loved. And since the dog-house was close enough to the back patio, this enabled her to play with them, which she liked to do.

Mom would sit on the front patio to catch the breeze and, sometimes, she would have questions and answers, like school, with our closest neighbours' children. One particular young boy was very bright, brighter than the other older boy, and she always said he was going to be a doctor, lawyer or scientist. That young boy grew up and is currently in China studying architecture; she would have been very proud of him.

I took Mom a few Sundays to worship at the Wesleyan Holiness Church (formerly the Pilgrim Holiness) on Popeshead and Bishopgates Streets, the same one we attended before migrating; and also to the Salvation Army when she initially came back home however, she much preferred to worship where I attended, The Science of Being (SOB) Temple of Light Love and Truth.

When I first arrived in Antigua I met with my friend Arlene Marsh and her sister, Marina Marsh, and was introduced to this concept. Her Grace, The Most Rev. Patricia Anita Limerick-Andries, Ph.D., is the founder, archbishop and messenger. Our teachings are about attaining self-mastery through practicing the *Principles of Light, Love, and Truth* and revealing the *Truth of Beingness* as we overcome our fears, doubts and condemnations.

Science is to know and Being is Self, and to be your highest and best self we become more aware of the Truth of Being = Man Know Thyself at all times.

Therefore, our teachings provide the platform for *Liberation of Consciousness*, and it is, in its right, a liberation theology. Our teachings are based on the inspirations of the ancient Masters of Light Love and Truth, channeled through our Beloved Messenger. Our teachings inspire us to go within one's self and take full responsibility for our thoughts, words and actions, self correct, and find our true and divine purpose.

Although the tunes to our songs are similar to those same choruses from the well-known *Sanky*, when they are sung to the amazing beat of drums, it pulsates in our entire body and gets us moving and shaking off all negativity.

Mom loved the drums and she would be jigging and having a great time. On fourth Sundays, we celebrate our cultural heritage, in wearing our African attire and accessories. She loved her African regalias and how we revere and remember our ancestors and pour libation for them using water. She did a lot of dancing to the drums on such Sundays in particular. These things brought her immense joy as she worshipped.

It was a pleasure to see her strum her hands as if playing a guitar when she jigged and danced to the rhythmic sound of the beat of the drums.

Mom's spiritual name was Master of Light (MOL) Survival. She was the oldest person in the Center and was therefore awarded the privilege of being the Queen Mother. This is to honour our elder mothers as a sign of respect and appreciation as the foundation of our Nation. Its origin is borne out of our African heritage in which mothers were highly respected as leaders of their societies.

Our Science of Being Queen Mothers have oversight of the attitude, behavior, and decorum of our members, and play their role by giving advice where necessary to improve the overall growth of all.

A Mother of the Church is an elder who has been caring, compassionate, loving, and morally upstanding in the community of the church and in the Society to which they belong. She is therefore qualified spiritually to counsel the members of the church if she observes that guidance is needed in any area of their livingness. They are the Dorcas Consciousness of the Ministry.

A Queen Mother of our Ministry is one who has reached the age of retirement – that is, 70-80 years – and who has been a Mother of the Church and now counsels the deacons, ministers and other leaders. She is consulted on matters relating to mature areas, where maternal instincts and experience are vital. They do the daily prayers for the leaders of the church and for the ministry at large.

Our ceremonies are set to bring about the importance of establishing within our communities the honouring of our elders and keeping our heritage strong.

An official coronation for Mom was performed at the Center, with family and friends in attendance. These included the Governor-General, Dame Louise Lake-Tack; her most famous adopted son, the Prime Minister, Dr. Hon. Winston Baldwin Spencer; and her adopted daughter Valerie Harris-Pole. It was an occasion to be remembered as she became "Queen Mother Survival," a role very well suited for her character, and she enjoyed it.

My musician partner Terry and I opened a restaurant and jazz club on Redcliffe Street after hosting a few jazz shows with overseas entertainers. At the Club, we brought in acts to include Bankie Banks from Anguilla and Carl Gusta from St. Lucia, to name just a couple. Mom was always in attendance, enjoying the entertainment, since she did not want to stay at home and miss the show. Our really good friends Ike Isaac and Marcus Christopher were very supportive and always in attendance and they would spend some time with her.

When our band, 3D Hardway, played at O'Jays Beach Bar in the south of the island, she was in attendance. She enjoyed hearing Bruce Harris sing and got a great kick when Terry played his bass and would dip down low and come back up. She would laugh and was happy. When she danced, she would imitate him and play guitar with her hands, too. Mom loved to dance and we had a great time dancing at home and when we were out. One of her dancing partners at the State Independence Banquet was Sir MacLean "King Short Shirt" Emanuel, who is like family to us and his wife Esther whom we called "Queen Esther." Sir McLean is a singer one of Antigua and Barbuda longest standing and most successful Calypsonian winning the most crowns ever. When they visited Canada on their honeymoon they spent time with us at our homes. Their visit with Mom was very good; she did her usual cook up and was very happy to have them.

***

We kept in touch with the rest of the family in Canada and the States quite often, by phone. I would call my brother Muhammad and Cousin Ineta, in particular, by Skype video calls, using the computer. Mom liked this very much – seeing her son and other family members as she spoke with them. She would send them kisses by kissing the computer monitor, and we would have such a laugh. We used this method of staying connected for years, right up until she passed.

On our last visit together to Canada she was eighty-six years old, and we had a great time with Muhammad, the grandchildren and great grandchildren, cousins and adopted family. It was winter time and we stayed with family, friends and Muhammad with his three youngest children – Yusuf, Safiyyah, and Imran. Yusuf was very good with Mom: He would put her boots on for her; the scarf, coat, gloves, everything; and he always helped her up and down the steps. She liked and appreciated it and just loved him oh-so-much more for the caring. We also spent some time with Alicia, Akil's Mom at their home with them and had a very good time.

When we left my adopted sisters Maggie and Norma's apartment for the airport, to return to Antigua, Mom cried kissing them goodbye and on the drive to the airport. Akil met us at the airport before we departed which she loved and was very happy to see him, we waved goodbye to him as we went through for boarding and as we got on the plane she cried again, telling me she might never see them again. Mom did see Akil when he and his family visited with us and she saw Muhammad twice when he came home to visit.

Mom met her most famous adopted son back in the nineties, when she would come down every year for a visit. My sister Valerie and her husband, Conrad, had a restaurant on Newgate Street called "Tropical Treat," and they had some of the best hamburgers in town. Mom used to visit there often; she would come to town by bus, if she had to, and go by to visit, then Terry or I would pick her up to go home. This is where she was introduced to Mr. Winston Baldwin Spencer, and she loved and admired him from then.

He was the leader of the United Progressive Party (UPP) and the Opposition Leader – at one time the only Opposition member in Parliament. Mom made it her business to always encourage him; she believed in him and prayed for him.

Mom's brother, Uncle Georgie, supported the UPP also, and we would all have political discussions. He was also one of our most-loved uncles. Mom listened to the Observer Radio every day, particularly "The Voice of the People" with Winston Derrick. She and Maxine, her caregiver, could tell me all that was said on the radio during the day, and at night and Saturdays she listened, with me, to "The Snake Pit" with Algernon 'Serpent' Watts whom she loved. We danced to the music he played before she went to bed especially on the Saturday nights. It was gratifying for me having these moments with Mom.

Prior to the 2004 election Talk radio was king that was the climate therefore Mom was not interested in watching TV she listened to the radio, specifically Observer and Crusader radios. She was a guest at the official Launch/opening of Crusader radio where Valerie would produce the news and sometimes present the news and on the weekends I would present the news and later on I hosted a program named "Facts not Fiction" Mom was always tuned in. She enjoyed listening to the UPP women on the radio Jacqui Quinn Leandro, Joann Massiah, D. Gisele Isaac and Joan Underwood she felt delighted and proud.

Sometimes she would call in on "The Voice of the People" and speak with Winston. On her bornday he would send her greetings and referred to her as his "ardent listener." She loved Winston Derrick and enjoyed listening to him. Leading up to the 2004 elections, we went to the rallies. Mom always wanted to go; she was not staying home. Most days, I was also out campaigning after I got home from work.

Just prior to election, on a Sunday while at work, I got a call from a church minister, who informed me that my uncle, George Adams, had collapsed in church and was on his way to the hospital. Uncle George had my name and number in his Bible in case of emergency.

I went to the hospital, where I found him unconscious. The Doctor informed me that he had a stroke. So I called his daughter Gloria in New York, and she came home within a few days. Then, about two days after her arrival, Uncle George passed away. We gave him a good send-off and we all cried, with Mom telling me that she would miss him, now that she had no more siblings, and it was just her, left alone in the world.

Mom and I believed we had the best family physician in Dr. Edmond Mansoor. Mom was comfortable with him and liked his service, and he soon became one of her "Loves." She did not miss her doctor in Canada. For not only did Dr. Mansoor give her a senior's discount, most times he did not charge her, at all, and she would bless him continually and keep him in her prayers.

He was our doctor for many years, until he took a break for politics and government service. We then started going to Dr. Sharon Cordner and she remained our family physician throughout.

I had some UPP paraphernalia, including some T-shirts, flyers, and posters that I was distributing in our neighbourhood. Mom picked out big posters of her adopted son, Dr. Spencer, and of Dr. Jacqui Quinn Leandro, and she had these posters plastered on her bedroom wall. She never removed them; they stayed there until she passed away and beyond.

I recall Mom being very proud on D-Day – Election Day 2004 – as she was going to cast her vote – specifically for the woman who was running in our constituency, Dr. Quinn Leandro.

The United Progressive Party (UPP) won the elections overwhelmingly, a landslide victory making history defeating the Antigua Labour Party and the Bird Family, who had run the Government for twenty-eight consecutive years. Dr. Quinn Leandro captured her seat by a very wide margin, making history as the first woman to be elected to Parliament in Antigua and Barbuda. Mom was related to the Hampson family on her Father's side they were related to the Adams from Winthrop village Blizard as she called, and also the Barnes. When she reconnected with Lady Mary Geo. Quinn in our neighbourhood at a Community function the Community group had put on and they talked and talked and hug up and kiss and trace the family back, thus making her related to Jacqui, this made her even more extremely proud of Jacqui and her winning the election.

Dr. Spencer became the Prime Minister; Willmoth Daniel, our former neighbour whom we grew up with, was now the Deputy Prime Minister; and my sister Valerie Harris Pole was now the Executive Assistant to the Prime Minister. It was a personal victory and triumphant experience for Mom.

After UPP won the election in 2004 we went to the first setting of Parliament and afterwards Mom expressed, on the landing before going down the stairs to leave and looking up in the skies to the Universe she started praying and giving thanks and she exclaimed "My Lord! A new Government UPP finally, I can die now" It was a surreal experience for her.

After that, Mom and I attended every Government function and UPP event. These included the Independence Banquet that the Party established in the "Homecoming" line-up, which it extended by adding many more activities and events. I too was a proud member of the Banquet Committee.

At our twenty fifth anniversary of Independence in 2006 Prince William was on island for the celebrations and attended our Independence State Banquet and Mom was fortunate, blessed and honoured to be in his presence which was incredible. She was touched and spoke of it on the drive home and how much she so loved his mother Princess Diana.

Mom never got bored or fell asleep when we were out during the Carnival festivities at night or in Parliament for the Throne Speeches or the Budget

Speeches, or the debates. Whatever the function, Mom was always alert, even though she was usually the oldest person in attendance.

On our way home she would tell me what she had liked; what she had enjoyed; whom she had met and spoken with; and who was nice, interesting, pretty, beautiful, or was wearing a great outfit. She did not remember everyone's name, but she could describe them in detail to me. And there was always someone new she would meet, or someone she knew already, and she would tell me she loved them.

I was now employed by the Government, first as the Deputy Coordinator in the Carnival office and the Secretary on the Carnival Development Committee (CDC) then the Acting Carnival Coordinator. The office and name was dissolved and the National Festivals Office (NFO) created with my position changed to Office Manager. Our execution of a magnificent and epic 50th Carnival celebrations, inspired Prime Minister Spencer with some encouragement from Valerie and I to play Mas' with us in "Revellers," the Mas' Band of Colin "Wanga" Martin. We would put on our costumes and headpieces and carry our standards, and whatever section we selected to play in, we led it including Vaughn Walter, Amb. Leon "Chaku" Symister and Johnson Browne.

We did this for many years, and our Band was always the most colourful and prettiest on the road. We won "Band of the Year" for fifteen consecutive years and more....

On Carnival Tuesday, Maxine and Mom would go to the Senior Citizens Tent, sponsored by Ludwick McDonald Reynolds (LMR) to watch the Parade. And when we got to the tent, they —and all the seniors — would be just waiting for us. We would step out of the band for a quick minute to greet them and take a photo. This made Mom happy, and all the seniors just loved it. They wanted to touch the Prime Minister and to have us stay longer with them.

***

My nephew Akil with his wife Camille and their first born Lauryn, visited with us here in Antigua for a week, it made Mom very happy. She was delighted to see one of her great-grandchildren — to hold her, kiss her up, and play with her every day. Mom was grateful, especially since Akil was the only grandchild that came down to visit with her. We all had a magical time together, creating everlasting memories.

Then my brother Muhammad came down – after forty-plus years of being away – and visited with us for a month. At this time, I took a vacation and went overseas, affording Mom and Muhammad quality time together.

She was so happy to have her son with her that, one time, as we were sorting out clothes to go out; she ended up pressing Muhammad's shirt. Now, Mom did not even press her own clothes; Maxine and I did that. And Muhammad could press his own shirt. But there she was, eighty-eight years old, and she put up the ironing board, got the iron, and went to work.

When I discovered this, and called Muhammad to see, he ended up just grinning. I asked Mom what she was doing and why, and she proceeded to tell me she was pressing her son's shirt because she knew how and she could.

At one point, Aunt Martha became very ill and was hospitalized for about a month, and we would visit her every day. When she was discharged, she still had health issues and needed to go to the out-patient clinic. But her husband, Uncle Kenneth, had died and she was living alone, and she could not look after herself. I therefore took her to my home, where Maxine, Mom and I cared for her.

Aunt Martha called Mom "Cousin May" even when they were both in their eighties, and she referred to Granny as "Aunt Lucy" (short for Louisa). Mom was very active in her care, including dressing Aunt Martha and looking after her hair – which was remarkable at her age – but she enjoyed looking after her as her younger sister.

Aunt Martha's son Bradley came down from London England and took her back with him a few weeks after. Mom cried for a couple of days after they left, and said to me that she might never see her again. This ended up being true, since she passed away in England around Christmas day, about six weeks after Mom passed.

Mom was blessed to live to see the first Black President of the United States, and that was a very big deal for her and a personal triumph. Watching the Inauguration on TV, she cried and gave praise and thanks to God. She had been watching the news and the debates and staying current, while saying prayers for Obama to win the election.

I embraced every opportunity to hone my acting skills and was blessed to work with some of the best Actors. Edson Bunting and the late greats George Rick James, Earl Goodwin and Vaughn Walter are a few and Meredith Mathurin including Hama production in their movies, and their TV soap of "Paradise View". Vaughn and I are two of the main characters featured in the movie "Once in an Island" and Mom was also an extra in a few of the scenes the Court room and in Parliament. It was a new experience for Mom and she enjoyed it.

Rick and I did a number of plays together and then we established the Radical Fringe Theatre made up of patrons Jasper "Bobby" Scotland and George Pigotts and we were the Co-producers. We met at my home a couple times each week and Rick would either prepare his famous chili or pizza that we had after the meetings and Mom would join us and we had some good laughs, she also knew his Mother from when they were young girls and she would always inquire about her from Rick and she attended her funeral when she passed.

In 2007 Rick wrote and directed "Our Country" a historical drama to commemorate the Abolition of the British Empire Atlantic Slave Trade which we had staged in April with a very large cast and a series of productions. Mom was very supportive and had her two cent worth to offer to us and encouragement always and she was in attendance at most of the productions.

CHAPTER 11

||||||||||||||||||||||||||||||||||||||||||||||||||||||||||||||||||||||||

THE FINAL CURTAIN

One Sunday morning in November 2009, when Mom was eighty-nine years old, I got up from my bed and went to her room to check on her. There, I found her on the floor, with her face twisting, etc., all indications that she was having a stroke. I immediately picked her up and put her to sit on her bed, then phoned my neighbour across the street, Nurse Charmaine Gouveia. She and I got Mom up walking and took her to the bathroom (where she said she had been going when she fell down). I called the ambulance and we got her to Mount St. John Medical Center (MSJMC).

Mom was hospitalized for a week, and I got permission to stay with her every night, sleeping in a chair. Maxine would come early in the mornings, and she stayed there with her, while I went home, cleaned up, and went to work. Then, after work, I would go back to the hospital to allow Maxine to leave; I would make a quick trip home and then back to stay until the morning. She also had family, church members, her adoptees Valerie and PM Spencer visit with her.

When Mom was discharged I had to get her a wheelchair, also my adopted sister Olive immediately shipped one down from Canada which was a commode that doubled as a wheelchair; a very strong one that today, after nine years, is still being utilized by my Aunt Mary.

I abandoned my bed and slept with Mom in hers; and every morning we would do the stretches and exercises that we were given. Mom then went through physiotherapy at MSJMC. I would take her and Maxine in the morning, and sometimes pick them up after, or get my taxi guy Wallace to take them home.

Maxine and Ms Barbara Bird, the Physiotherapist, would tell me that Mom was very entertaining when exercising, and she and Maxine would also help out with the others patients. When she rode the bicycle she would tell them that she was going to ride to Willikies (a village on the Northeastern end of the island), then she would make other pronouncements that she was now passing Parham or Pares Village. And when she finally arrived in Willikies, she would shout out that she had reached and clap her hands.

Olive came down to visit with us in January, right around Mom's ninetieth bornday. I had planned a bornday celebration for her and had a good venue that I decorated nicely. Muhammad came down from Canada, and my sisters, Una Hayles from Canada and Una Simon, and her daughter, Paula, came in from Trinidad for the occasion. Mom was unable to make a grand entrance by walking into her ninetieth bornday celebration; however, she was wheeled in style, by her son and daughter, her two youngest children.

The occasion was well attended by a hundred and ten family members; church family; and close friends, including Governor-General Dame Louise Lake-Tack; Prime Minister Spencer and Mrs. Jacklyn Spencer; Finance Minister Harold Lovell; and President of the Senate Dame Hazlyn Mason Francis.

It was celebrated in worship, giving praise and thanks, as we sang and clapped and had the beat of the drums. We had plenty of entertainment – Shiva School of Dance, solo renditions, and keyboard performances, plus speeches with a great emcee, her nephew, Peter Gordon.

When Prime Minister Spencer, her adopted son, got up to the podium and started to deliver his speech, Mom jumped out of the wheelchair all on her own. She held onto the handles and started to smile, acknowledging him. She shocked everyone in attendance, since we did not know she could even move like that on her own; but with pure delight and determination she did. And after oohing and aahing and exhaling, everyone applauded her.

Mom strived well and basically made a full recovery, and she was once again able to take care of herself, for the most part.

One day, while my friend and our Church sister Ileater Christian were visiting with her, Mom told her to come close. She said to her, "I am adopting you. You are my good friend that I can tell you things in confidence." She told Ileater that she loved her husband and their daughter, too, and how much she admired them. And she advised them to continue to take care of themselves and to look good. "People don't know what you have in your stomach, because they can't see; but they can see what you have on, so always look good," and keep trusting in God, Mom told her.

A few months later, in October, Mom had a second stroke. Her caregiver Maxine also fell ill, and Ileater, too, became very sick ending up in the ICU at MSJMC while Mom was on the regular ward. Maxine had suffered a few Tran's ischemic attacks (TIA) and was under the doctor's care during that time. She then had a stroke and died.

This was unexpected, heart-breaking and devastating for her children and grandchildren, since Maxine was only forty-eight years old. She had become part of our family for nine years, the length of time she had spent in Antigua. Whenever I had to travel, she would move in with her two youngest children and her grandson and care for Mom until my return.

Maxine and her children also worshipped with us at the SOB Center and she was a member. She lived in Prime Minister Spencer's constituency, and supported the UPP. She and the children had attended the rallies with us and she had worn her blue T-shirt with pride. Whenever I was late getting home from work, I would drive her home; it gave Mom an outing and fresh air, which she liked.

Maxine had developed herself professionally as a caregiver. With some assistance from me, she had taken a private course in "Caring for the Elderly" and graduated with honours. Her children, Mom and I had attended her graduation; we were very proud of her and took lots of pictures.

She had gone on a diet and lost a lot of weight, after which she had cut off her dreadlocks and started wearing wigs, make-up and lipstick. Mom and I would sometimes tease her about her new look and improved image, and tell her that she was really "looking out." But I encouraged her and helped her along since it was good seeing this transformation in her.

When Mom came home from the hospital this second time I had no one to care for her. It was a very bad struggle trying to find someone suitable, so I had to fully care for her myself. Plus, for a few months, I did not tell her that Maxine had died, because of her own condition.

I decided to bring someone from Dominica to live-in with us and care for Mom; but that did not work out well, because the person was not caring or kind. So I had to find someone else – which I did – a very nice lady from Jamaica; so I parted company with Ms. Dominica.

The lady from Jamaica, Claudia Walters, moved in with us to care for Mom. She was very good with her and Mom loved her, also. But Mom would keep asking about Maxine, and I had to eventually tell her that Maxine had died. She cried for Maxine and was never the same after.

I would bring Maxine's daughter, Stacy, and two of her grandchildren to spend weekends with us. They took over my bedroom, because I slept with Mom, and they were all over Claudia's room, also – because that was where they were accustomed to being when Maxine was alive and they came over to spend time with Mom. But Claudia was very accommodating and loved Stacy.

I would take Mom driving in the country to get fresh air and to have some activities. Sometimes we went to the mall; I put her in her wheel chair and push her about, especially when Claudia was on her days off on the weekends. We were in our Center for worship every Sunday with her in the wheelchair.

We celebrated Mom's ninety-second bornday in February, and we had relatives, church family and friends come by to celebrate with us. I dressed her up nicely in a very regal outfit and placed her in the wheel chair, and she was greeted by the children first then everyone else. When she was tired and I had to take her back to her room to undress and lie down, she asked me to wait; and she told everybody, "I really love you; I love everybody."

Claudia had a twin sister in Jamaica who came to Antigua with a friend for a three-week visit and stayed with us. Then Muhammad came back down and spent a month with us; and he did an excellent job of helping us take care of Mom. He read to her, took her onto the patio for air, and took a lot of pictures.

During Mom's illness, she had lots of family and friends who would visit with her our cousins Marilyn James-Simon; Juanita James; Winston Gordon; and Keith Hamilton, Dame Louise Lake Tack, the Governor-General; and her son, Prime Minister Spencer, always took the time to come by, making her day delightful.

***

Mom was accustomed to having manicures and pedicures, and we would always go together to get them done. When she got sick, I would then pick up the nail technician and bring her to our home to do Mom's nails, and this I kept up until a week and a half before her passing.

Mom was very loving, kind, friendly, outgoing, passionate, funny, sophisticated, and magnetic. She loved to dress-up and have things coordinated: her stockings, hat, scarfs, gloves, purse and shoes. She was self-confident, self-reliant, graceful and very independent, compassionate and courageous. She would try some unexpected things surprising you just for the experience, and she could also drive a car.

Mom is from humble beginnings and she instilled humility in us. She had a very big heart, a great forgiving soul, and a sweet spirit. She was generous, always giving and doing things for people. When someone from her work place was sick, she would make chicken soup and bread pudding and then take the bus or subway to deliver it to them. She taught us to help family and others; to be content with what we had and then work towards achieving better; and that "nothing happens before its time." She also encouraged us never to be too disheartened, because whatever the situation, it will not last, it will pass, and it will change and to pray about everything and believe.

In her years of volunteering, Mom witnessed a lot of suffering and sick people who had no family to visit them in the hospital. When they died, she would go to the funeral because, as she said, "they didn't have anybody." She said everybody needs love and care, and family was the most important thing, so we should not hold things in our hearts against each other.

Mom was an exceptional person with an extraordinary character and a sweet soul with a wonderful Spirit. She was a teacher, a nurse, guidance counselor, an inspiration and motivator. She taught us to be kind and said that when someone was kind to us we must always reciprocate; find a way to give back. For example, their Birthday or when it was Christmas time we should give that person a gift, or even a card. She kept greetings cards all the time, as stock in her drawer: Thank you; Get well; Sympathy, Birthday and Christmas cards.

Mom kept small quantities of money in her possession, such as five-dollar bills; and she would put the money into the hands of family members, children and adults, including adopted members and their children. Sis Betty John at Mom's burial spoke of her squeezing her hand and when you looked it was a five dollar bill, in addition she spoke of Mom teaching her to make 'black cake' but she never quite got it. My young cousins from the "James family" talk about getting their five dollar bills squeezed into their hands; this is how they remembered her for the kindness and generousity she displayed.

Mom was terrified of Dentist because when she was younger and went to a Dentist called "Wisenger" for an extraction; he was horrible and made her face swell up etc. This propelled her to take very good care of her teeth; she would brush after eating each meal and took her tooth brush and tooth paste on the job with her daily to enable her to brush her teeth after lunch. She basically had all her teeth in place and our Dentist Dr. Derrick Marshall was good with her and she loved him because he didn't make her feel any pain even for a filling.

Mom knew colours and materials very well and all the varied shades of colour of which she tried to teach me. She said material had to breathe especially in the heat you wear cotton, gabardine and linen. She knew poplin, peau de soie, banlon, satin, chiffon, gabardine, percale crepe, sateen and velvet. We would argue about colours she said I mixed them up and I didn't know the difference between beige and cream, I knew one was lighter than the other and we would laugh about it.

Mom was a trailblazer in many aspects of her life and in her church. She also said it is good to have friends from all walks of life. For example, your living-room friend is not going to come into the kitchen to help you out, and vice versa, she would explain. She was happy being with the highest and the lowest, socially, and she could sit and converse with kings and queens and paupers. She would instill in me – even in adulthood – as did my Dad, that I was "not better than anyone, but no one else was better than me." And she always stressed the golden rule, "Do unto others as you would have them do unto you." Even after she had experienced, prejudice, racism and degradation. She had another thing she used to say "Every dog has his day and every pussy has his night."

Another of her adoptees that she loved, appreciated and admired was Inspector Trevor Young who was always helpful and respectful.

Mom had to make some hard choices throughout her journey in life, and those decisions are still beneficial to us. She grasped the opportunities that were presented to her to improve her life and those of her children and family.

She strongly believed in prayer and prayed constantly and believed her prayers were always going to be answered. She had great faith.

She was a virtuous woman and we all grew up and called her blessed.

***

Mom was ready to meet her maker and be in the Promised Land as she expressed to me, I then released her unto her God self and she made her transition, dying in ease and in peace in the early morning of November 7, 2012, after President Obama had been declared the winner in the US election, giving him a second term. The matriarch, Queen Mother, Mom took her rest less than three months away from her ninety-third bornday.

I organized a memorial service in Antigua for Mom, and then I went to Canada for her burial at Mount Pleasant Cemetery, where her plot had already been paid for many years ago, and at her request. I had her remains shipped back to Canada for burial with her son Patrick.

My brother Lloy had flew over from Miami and was with Muhammad, the grandchildren, great-grandchildren, family members, her adopted children and friends were present at the graveside for her interment. Her grandson Akil arranged to have some doves for us to send into flight, as well as a repast at his home, which I know she would have liked. I believe she was very pleased and was smiling down at us from the cosmos, or whatever celestial realm she is on.

Since Mom's passing, her first adopted daughter and my best friend, Valerie Harris Pole passed in 2015, and then two more of her birth children died in 2017, six weeks apart. My sister Joan was first. Muhammad and I sojourned to England to support her only child, Eon, and assist with the funeral arrangements. Joan is buried there.

With my brother Lloy, in Miami, Muhammad and I were both there when he took his last breath. We assisted his daughter Veronica with the arrangements and had him cremated; then we brought his ashes back to Canada and laid him to rest with Mom and Pat.

Muhammad and I are the only two left now.

***

I still love, admire, and respect my Mom, and thank the universe for the blessing she has been to me; and I am grateful that it was her womb that was selected to bring me forth.

You could not be in Mom's presence without her saying a kind word to you, paying you a compliment, or giving you a little joke to make you smile or laugh. Her mantra was calling you "Picknee" and telling you that she "lub you whole tun" – that she loved you a whole ton.

Mom's days were so much fuller and richer in her golden years, as she lived her best life.

This was Mom's life journey and how she evolved as a person, with such a character, soul, and lovely spirit.

Mom – Veronica Elizabeth Adams-Tully – has left three generations of Canadians from her lineage. If Mom had not made several sacrifices over the years, specifically, leaving her children behind and then eventually migrating to Canada, these grandchildren, great-grandchildren and great-great grandchildren would not be there today. She also has six Grandchildren in the States and great grandchildren; these and all the things she has done for others remain her legacy.

I know for sure that when the Ancestors saw Mom and ask her "What she did with their sacrifices?" She can boldly and proudly respond that she took every advantage of them with pride and dignity; that she lived her life with love and respect for them; that she operated with their indomitable spirit within and she revered them.

I know if Mom was alive and well she would not have missed our "Island Girls" arriving back home in Antigua from rowing across the channel our Ancestors travelled, she would have been front and center to greet them and I believe that she was present with them in Spirit and at their home coming waving her Antigua and Barbuda flag with pride.

In life when you are saved from bad situations and circumstances you need to remember that someone or persons prayed for you, these persons made tremendous sacrifices through blood, sweat, and tears for you. When you are enjoying freedom, rights, and the good things in life, someone paved the way; they blazed the trail for you and you ought to be grateful. They are to be respected, honoured and revered.

When you die what legacy will you leave, what you will say to the Ancestors when they ask you what did you do with their sacrifices.

***

I wrote this poem for Mom and women I admired in 2005 in Antigua and had it published in the Observer newspapers for Mother's day.

WOMEN OF WORTH

Women who are spirit filled
Women of quality consciousness
Women of substance
Women of antiquity
Women of pride
Women full of confidence
Women of principle
Women of grace
Women with love, order, organization and efficiency
Women with testicular fortitude to meet and defeat challenges
Women that rise above adversity and the odds
Women of accomplishment
Women that have and continue to give of themselves unselfishly to family,
friends, community, and country with much grace and dignity
Women in our community and of our Country
Women deserving of praise and recognition
Women I love, admire, and respect
I salute you Women:
Veronica Elise Adams-Tully
Rev. Patricia A. Limerick-Andres
Valerie Harris-Pole
Bishop Hazel Luke
H. E. Louise Lake-Tack
Dame Yvonne Maginley
Veronica Carlos
Monica Dear
Cheryl Carter
Bondalyn Adams
Hon. Dr. Jacqui Quinn-Leandro

Sen. Joanne Massiah
Keva Margetson
Hazelyn Francis
D. Gisele Isaac-Arrindell
Joanne Hillhouse
Mitzi Allen
Cleon Athill
Valerie Hodge
Denise Francis

By
Patricia Louisa Tully, CHE

THANK YOU MOTHER

Though these words may not be ample,
I know love through Your example.
The consistency of your love
Is like no other
My teacher,
My guide,
My Mother.

Anonymous.

MOTHER'S

Mother's everybody has one
There are Mother's and then
There are Mother's and there
Will be Mother's
Mine is the best of all the rest
That may not be true to you
But to me, my Mother is a soul in bliss

In all eternity.
May Allah reward you with a Godly reward
And grant you his mercy, blessing and peace
I Love you Mom and will forever miss you.

Your son
Muhammad.
Written in November 2012 after her passing.

A TRIBUTE TO MOTHERS-MY MOTHER

Put aside all dogmas religious and otherwise. Be it Judaism doctrine, Christianity doctrine or
Islamic doctrine. And all the other philosophical teachings regarding Parents, particularly Mothers.
In life there is an indisputable fact a reality in every sense of the word and throughout human history which will very well continue until the end of the human species is-A Woman who becomes a Mother.
Allow me to clarify what I mean by Mother. A woman who is pregnant carries the unborn child
through all the stages of gestation healthfully and otherwise, more often with many difficulties, and
eventually though always painful gives birth to a child be it male or female. You listen to the Joyous
exclamation of both mother and child and those who witness the birth! This is the first stage though very paramount to being a mother.
A woman who gives birth sometimes by choice other times because of vicious circumstances chose
to outsource the early development or raising of the child. Allah and history will judge that choice?
However, most other women will elect as difficult it is to raise the child to maturity and beyond. The
endeavor requires most of all Love and, Compassion. To care, to nature, to provide and protect, these actions create an unbreakable bond between the caregiver and the child. That is the definition of a Mother. A Mother doesn't

necessarily have to give birth to gain the distinction or qualification of being a Mother! A woman of Love and Compassion as shown over and over again throughout human history who devoted herself to the raising and development of a child or children to maturity

is a qualified Mother, she enjoys the rank of Motherhood.

I am oh so Bless to have "Loved Woman" who not only gave me birth but who stuck around regardless of the difficulties to raise me up from a state of helpless to maturity, to manhood!

The Glory and Praise belong to the Creator of all things, Allah, The Almighty. May Our Lord Bless and Reward Our Dear Mother with Paradise! Peace and Blessings upon my

Mother. Peace and Blessing on all the Messengers and Prophets of Allah. Peace be upon all for

reading and listening, my humble gratitude to you on behalf of my Mother.

> Peace and Love
> A Son of Veronica Tully
> Muhammad Hadi Abdullah – written February 5, 2020

***

SHARING SOME TESTIMONIALS TO MY MOTHER'S GOOD QUALITIES

"Mom is the most loving person I have ever met."

"Mom's love was expressive; she showed you she loved you with words, kisses, embraces, huge tight hugs, touches on the arms, shoulders or wherever; and listening to you."

"She was a consummate lady; a quintessential lady; she made you feel like you were the only important person without offending others. She embodied confidence, sophistication, grace, dignity and a wonderful Spirit. She was a very bright Light, which she carried with distinction for all to see."

"Mom was a trailblazer and laid many foundations .... She was a beautiful woman inside and out."

"Mom is the only person I have known that personifies the example of Jesus the Christ ... with the principles and examples He has left us to live by."

"There is so much I could say about Mrs. Tully affectionately known as Mom. My recollection is a lady who had so much love it just poured out of her. Mom was a true Christian I know she is in Haven with her Lord, she was one of the most stylist women and it was my privilege to know her" Una Hayles.

"Mrs. Veronica Tully or Mom Tully as I'd call her was a very lovely lady indeed. Her kind and hospitable manner was not one I could forget after our initial meeting at a church function. She had already adopted my brother Michael so it was easy to include me as family. She spoke regularly of her own six children but in her heart there was always space to adopt one more child. Being away from my own family, a young woman migrating to a strange land, she ensured I was adjusting to the new land, people and culture. She tutored me on how to dress for the changing weather from season to season, shopped with or for me sometimes with her own earnings. Mom Tully loved the Lord Jesus Christ and that was the main connection that drew us together. She lived a life to please her Lord and we encouraged each other to the end of her days whether we were near or afar. Rest--in-Peace Mom Tully!

Louie, Lisa, Patricia, Mom's biological daughter returned from the USA to be closer to her mom. I must mention Olive, another adopted daughter who was very special to mom but to whom I did not often meet. We later found out that mom would at times shop for the same clothe item but in different colors for the three of us. Yes, not five but three of us. The girls' relationship grew stronger because of the fine lady in our lives Mrs. Veronica Tully."

TRIBUTE TO MOM

I knew Mrs Veronica Tully from Pilgrim Holiness Church on Bishopgate Street ever since I was around 6/7yrs old.

I was always with my Mom and Dad, who taught us to respect everyone, so we shared a lot of respect and conversations between our families.

Mrs Tully and her family sat immediately behind my family in church and we knew each other very well.

Lisa Tully and I have been the best of friends for years; we even dated and lived together for many many years, and moved to Antigua in the late 80s, where we celebrated life together. We migrated to Canada as teenagers around the same time and we still remain friends.

Mother Tully, affectionately called Mom by the folks she cared for and who cared for her. She was a very eccentric personality, loves dressing elegantly, loves people, loves to laugh, and enjoys dancing and telling old time stories. A very principled and expressive Christian woman, who is not afraid to speak her mind. She always showed me much love and respect, in spite of the kind of relationship I share with her daughter Lisa, a very caring woman.

I used to have conversations with Mom about anything, living life and what it feels like to be a senior. She used to enjoy coming out with her daughter to watch me play on Sundays when I played at OJ's. I would perform for her with my little stage moves that thrilled her and bring a little enjoyment and excitement to her Sunday evening outings.

Mom was a very forgiving woman, who I loved very much. She was full of life, and loved her Sunday mornings to dress up for church, to worship her Heavenly father. I had the privilege of giving back a little to Mrs Veronica Tully, by caring for her a little bit in her last few years!

Terry Lewis.

A REMARKABLE PRESENCE- VERONICA TULLY – OUR MASTER OF LIGHT SURVIVAL

I saw and interacted with a Life that was expressions of Love, Courage, Fearlessness and Action, even as she journeyed in her Nineties: Veronica Tully- the Unforgettable Presence.

The will to demonstrate that life was to be lived, as she danced, even in the moments when she was not at her best physical mobility. Her Rhythm was that of confidence and pure appreciation for life's offerings of music and its theatrics.

... I recall vividly that when she had her first bout of challenge, and she had to be confined to the wheelchair to get to the Temple on a Sunday morning, she expressed a manner of spiritual determination and strength of character. She sat quietly as the drums played, tapping her fingers on the tip of the chair, and slightly moving her head to the beat; when, all of a sudden, she stood up, without assistance, and moved out of the chair, with her hands in a guitar-playing stance, and bounced intently to the beat of the drums. It was amazing! We were in awe! And then she sat when she was fully satisfied!

Master of Light Survival is our eternal ancestor, for she inspired a determination in all of us that life is to be lived, expressed in Love and appreciation of everyone who enters our space. She did this every time one entered her company, and I was a recipient of her "Ah Love Me Love You" mantra of affection, and the kiss came with it all the time.

Ms. Tully was, indeed, an endearing personality, and you had no choice but to return the flurry of smooches and hugs; as now as I write this short memoir, I feel her presence!

She will remain in our Shrine forever as the Spirit of Endearment who taught each of us how to not take life so seriously, yet be respectful, kind and loving.

May your journey in the Spirit Realm continue to be encountered with Light angels and celestial beings, as we keep your memory of being one of the most loving presences that walked among us.

The Right Rev. Dr. Hazel Luke, Bishop

QUEEN MOTHER TULLY was a Soul Personality who exuded WARMTH, CARING, COMPASSION AND UNCONDITIONAL Love to all whom she met, and these fine Qualities are what endeared her to all of us in the Science of Being Center, of which she was a Member, and even to those persons who came in contact with her for the first time.

She was an example to those who are Seniors, because she participated in everything, and was at Worship every Sunday, dancing around in her seat when she felt the movement of the Spirit. Everyone looked forward to her coming through the door, dancing into the church, even when she was not on time. It was a joy to have her with us, and a joy for me to visit her for the wisdom and encouragement which she always had for persons sitting with her.

I have never seen her cross nor annoyed with anyone to the extent that she sulked. She was one of the most peaceful, motherly, kind-hearted Soul Personalities I have known besides my Grandmother, and I know that her Soul Substance is doing the same in the Thereafter, because she was a Genuine Consciousness of Divine Love among all wherever she went, and is a LIVING MEMORY of Graceful Dressing and Modeling of the Higher Self within this Ministry.

Her Grace Patricia Limerick-Andries, Ph.D.

IN REQUIEM

Was life worth living and indeed worth remembering? That definitely depends upon the individual.

Mother Tully who would have lived a worthy, worthwhile, rewarding and exemplary life, must be remembered not only for the life she lived but perhaps even more importantly, the lives she would have positively impacted beyond her immediate and extended family.

I am living testimony of a woman who loved, cared, defended and indeed supported my endeavours, my hopes, my aspirations for a better and more just Antigua and Barbuda. Even in my mature adult life, Mother Tully was indeed a genuine and sincere mother, friend and confidant.

Her memory lives on and her loving, caring and genuine support will never be forgotten and for me will not be interred with her bones.

Continue to rest, Mother Tully, in the everlasting arms of Almighty God.

W. Baldwin Spencer
Your "Son"

FAMILY TREE

||||||||||||||||||||||||||||||||||||||||||||||||||||||||||||||||||||

VERONICA ELIZABETH ADAMS-TULLY

Mother: Louisa Audain She had four children and later married **Hercules Buckley**
Theodore H Finch
Delores Finch
Veronica Elizabeth Adams
Agatha Adams
Father: Thomas Adams he had
- Eunice Adams
- George Adams
- **Veronica Elizabeth Adams**
- Agatha Adams

Walter Leslie Tully - Line

The **TOMLINSON** family name originates in Sussex, England.

FIRST GENERATION
Richard Tomlinson (an Englishman, itinerant saddler and shoemaker, living in Antigua at the time) of Newfield Village.
Abigail Joseph (daughter of freed African hostages (Richard Joseph and his wife) - commonly referred to as slaves - owned by Nathaniel Gilbert at Gilbert Estates).
Abigail's parents were married on the back steps of the Great House at Gilbert Estates. The marriage of Richard to Abigail was reputedly one

of the first inter-racial marriages in Antigua. Abigail was said to be very, very tiny.

(Source: Pedigree of Richard and Abigail Tomlinson – National Archives of Antigua document)

They had fifteen (15) children including twins. The children had different shades some were black, some light skin and some were white. One light skin Daughter was:

Georgiana Elvira *"Ma Lady"* Tomlinson she married Matthew George Davis of Newfield they had
- Herman *"Ernest"* Augustus Frederick
- Molly Davis (twin of Ultima Davis) had her first three children then left the country and had four other children
- Ultima *"Aunt Dada"* Davis (twin of Molly Davis) – She married Mr. Hilman in the USA.
- Clayton Davis (1st)
- Jacob Davis
- Miriam Davis

Molly Davis had her first three children
- Harold Scholar
- Avril Scholar
- **Walter Leslie Tully**

Tully originates in Ireland

William Tully and Susanna Olive Chatham-Tully had Leslie Tully and he had **Walter Leslie Tully and Kendrick Tully in Antigua and then six more children in the USA**

Veronica Elizabeth Adams married Walter Leslie Tully Children:
1. Theodore Patrick
2. Lloy Wendell
3. Joan Panelope
4. Clayton Leslie Aliston
5. Walton Arthur Leslie Tully aka Muhammad Hadi Abdullah

6. Patricia Louisa

Lloy's – Daughter – Veronica Wade; Granddaughter – Stephanie

Joan – Son – Eon Wade

Clayton – Son – Corey; Daughters – Chatoni and Chanta Tully

Walton/Muhammad –

– Kenneth and Yolanda Tully, Nichole Generette, Addie Tully, Akil Bishop Tully, Yusuf, Saffiyah and Imran Abdullah.

Walton's line starting with Kenneth Cornwall Tully he has:

1. **Omari** – he has – Rocharn, Omari Jr. Shevori; Wade and Suriyah
2. **Kenita** – has a son –Kayson
3. Latisha
4. Ezekiel
5. Jahesha
6. Jaliyah
7. Jasiah
8. Jaheim
9. Dwight – step
10. Jason – step
11. Tevin – step

Nichole Generette-Harvey has – one daughter Joy.

Adewale "Addie" Olusegun Tully has two daughters

Akil Banjoko L. E. Bishop has one son – David, three Daughters – Lauryn, Eva and Victoria

Yusuf Abdullah has one Daughter, Saffiyah Panelope, one son – Abdal Haleem Abdullah.

Imran Abdullah has one son - Zaden Abdullah.

Clayton's line:

Corey Tully has all boys – Corey Jr., Camoroy, Torey and Jacory Tully

Chatoni Tully-Washington has – Taveres, Tony and her Daughter Chaniel Washington

Chanta Tully-Jones has – Tanayjah, Terranique and Harmony Jones.

Adopted Children Kenneth Evanson, Carlton Green, Valerie HarrisPole (deceased), Conrad Pole, Ceceile Harris-Porter, Brenda Harris-Ephraim,

Charles Harris, Millicent McKinon-Gonsalves-Barreiro, Rudolph Davis, Ursula Moore, Dr. Winston Baldwin Spencer, Micheal and Elaine Fisher, Una Fisher-Simon, Wakefield Simom, Olive Isaacs, Una Hayles, Norma Beckford, Maggie Daniel-Manson, Betty John (deceased), Myrna Newman, Terry Lewis, Eudelyn Lewis, Ileater Christian, Relton Christian, Hazel Luke, Alicia Bishop-Messado, Ursula Moore, Maxine King and Trevor Young.

Adopted Grand Children Petra Bishop, Charmaine Joseph, Stacy Nicholas-Coleman, and Alizia Benjamin, Celeste Christmas-Smith.

Walter Leslie Tully of the Tomlinson Family on his Mother's side is related to the following:
Edward William Sigmund "*Siddy*" Tomlinson
DOB: 18 Sep 1865
Georgina Williams of Fall River, Nova Scotia - She was the daughter of Robert Williams (DOD: 08 Jan 1904 (66 yrs.)) and Charlotte Johnson DOD: 26 Dec 1905 (35 yrs)
Remarks: Georgina Williams was a 1st cousin of **William Neilson Edward Hall, VC.** (i.e. Georgina's mother, **Charlotte (Johnson) Williams** and William Hall's mother, **Lucinda (Johnson) Hall** were sisters. **William Neilson Edward Hall, VC** was the first black person, the first Nova Scotian and one of the first Canadians to receive the British Empire's highest award for bravery, the Victoria Cross.
The Downey relatives of Nova Scotia are descendants of Edward William Sigmund "*Siddy*" Tomlinson.

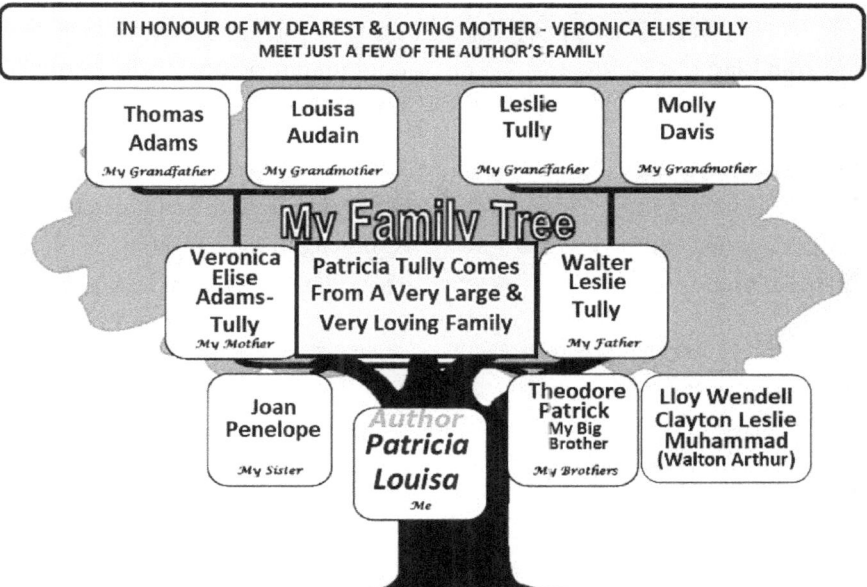

IN HONOUR OF MY DEAREST & LOVING MOTHER - VERONICA ELISE TULLY
MEET JUST A FEW OF THE AUTHOR'S FAMILY

Thomas Adams
My Grandfather

Louisa Audain
My Grandmother

Leslie Tully
My Grandfather

Molly Davis
My Grandmother

My Family Tree

Veronica Elise Adams-Tully
My Mother

Patricia Tully Comes From A Very Large & Very Loving Family

Walter Leslie Tully
My Father

Joan Penelope
My Sister

Author
Patricia Louisa
Me

Theodore Patrick
My Big Brother

Lloy Wendell Clayton Leslie Muhammad
(Walton Arthur)
My Brothers

VERONICA

From an island
In Antigua

She journeyed alone
With a single luggage
Of courage and skill
To make home proud

Her children were
pillars of love and gifts

So she cried
when she lost a son
Fought hard to heal
That hole in her heart

Yet never stopped
Holding unto God
For comfort
Strength...,

She became a volunteer
Making people happy
showed more love
To strangers

Until Dementia sets in
And stole her away
Forgetting she was
Was the people's love.

You brought victory
You brought kindness

The tears you wiped
With your cloth of compassion
And successes will always
live in the pages of our hearts.

Poem by Uche Uwadinach

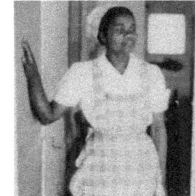

Early years in Antigua. Large pics are mom's wedding pic, and pictures with all her children. Smaller pics are mom in uniform where she worked, passport pic in dark dress and white dress pic is Christmas card mom sent to family and friends.

Early years in Canada.

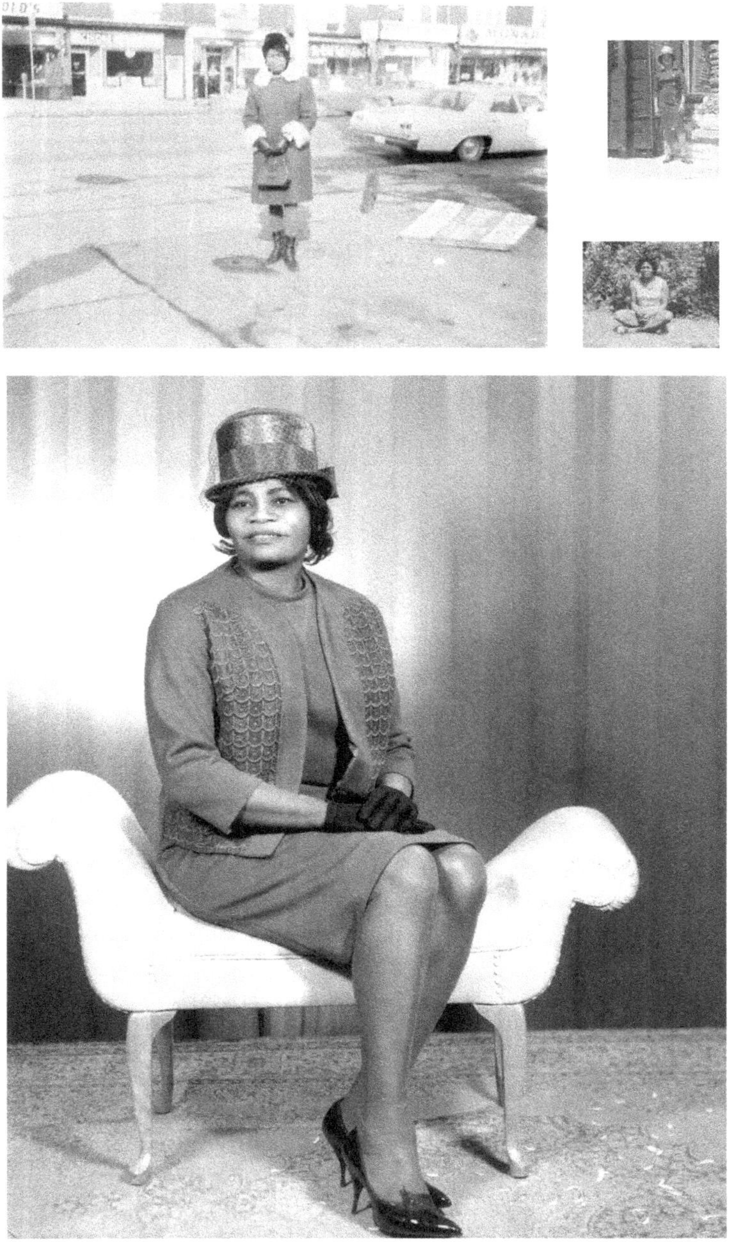

Mom and Lisa with son Patrick at his graduation from UFT
Bottom pic is mom dad Lisa and brother Moe

3 generations, son, 4 grandsons, and 7 great grandchildren.

Mom accepting volunteer service award over 10 years.

Mom in London and Paris with Lisa.

Mom's 90th celebrations, pic includes mom great great grandchild

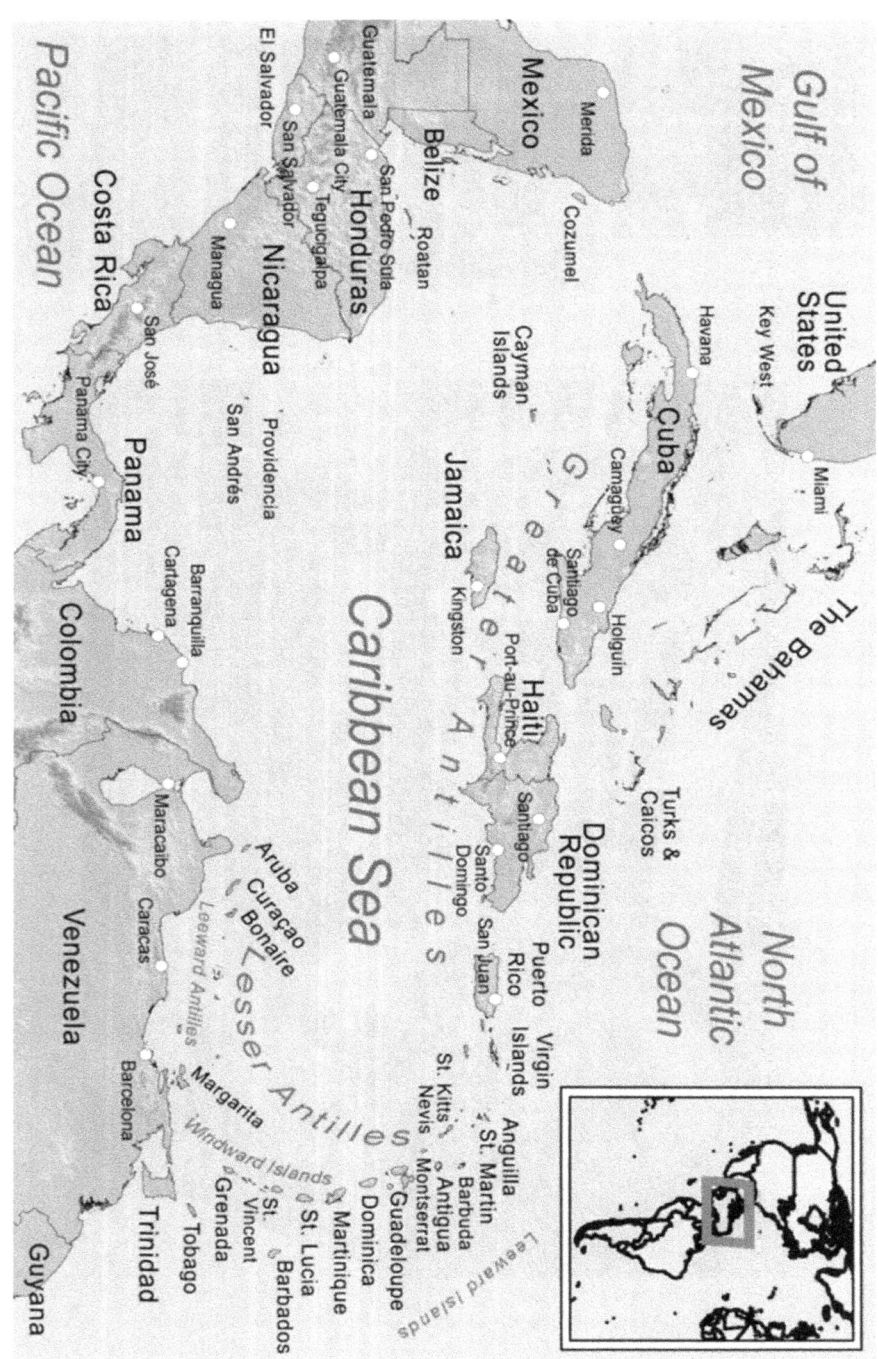

ACKNOWLEDGEMENTS

||||||||||||||||||||||||||||||||||||||||||||||||||||||||||||||||||||||||||||||||||||||||||||||||||||

I am giving thanks for my Mother Veronica first for bringing me forth and for the way she raised us and all the life lessons she has taught us, for her intuition, courage, love, compassion, resilience, independence, hard work, her unwavering faith and the lovely Spirit she possessed that has made me the woman that I am.

Thanks to my coauthor Ingrid for being the impetus that got me writing about Mom which was always my intention. Thanks to my Brother Muhammad for his encouragement as well as to his surprise that I do remember so much and also details; also for his poems and providing me with pictures of Mom.

To my family, relatives and friends thank you. My Cousin Yvonne, affectionately known as Ineta for her foreword and available family tree design. To Olive Isaac for her foreword and encouragement, and my Cousin Juanita James for knowing and confirming a particular material I had problems remembering and the accurate spelling. Thanks to Terry Lewis for confirming places and addresses in Toronto vital to the story.

Thanks to Paddy the "Griot" Simon for allowing me to pick his brains on facts and memories in Antigua, and Thanks to Dame D. Gisele Isaac-Arrindell for editing with respect and love.

Thanks for the contribution in testimonials of The Right Rev. Dr. Hazel Luke, Her Grace Patricia Limerick-Andries, PhD. Dr. Winston Baldwin Spencer, Una Simon, Una Hayles and Terry Lewis.

I give thanks to the Creator of all Creations of this Universe for the health, strength, focus, inspiration and the determination provided me in completing this project.

My purpose and objective to tell this story was to inform and examine an important issue in immigration as not only an act of love but as a legacy for my family and for the ethnic and immigrant community to use as a guide and learning tool.

To each of you I call forth abundant blessings and enrichment in your lives for taking the time to read, learn, and grow from this story.

Sincerely
Patricia Louisa Tully

CONCLUSION

||||||||||||||||||||||||||||||||||||||||||||||||||||||||||||||||||

It was a pleasure and a great learning experience for both Patricia and I to embark on this journey of exploration into the life of our parents and their decision to venture into new territories.

It became not only a lesson in our heritage and culture but also a spiritual and emotional journey. We initially thought it would be a quick evolution that would take perhaps two or three weeks out of our present day reality to put on paper but instead we were forced to take time to reflect, to look both forward and backwards into where we are , where we came from, and where we were meant to be.

It took us to a new reality and place that made us truly grateful for who we are and where we are from. It taught us to be even more steadfast in our daily life and to accept our struggles as life lessons. It further presented to us a new reality and a realization that no matter what befalls us we had a responsibility to carry on the torch that was passed on to us. We had been given an amazing example and blueprint that we could not ignore or take for granted.

Our mothers had shown us that it did not matter what humble beginnings you were handed out at birth determination, ambition and the desire to do well were the driving tools behind survival and success. As well as the never ending belief in something or someone greater than what was obvious in our day to day living. Both women were women of strong faith who persevered.

Veronica chose to do it alone without her husband but had help from her older sons in crossing the Atlantic Oceans. Dolvis initial and early help came from her oldest daughter Joy and stepson Keith. Teamwork and family were the building blocks of these early pioneers.

Patricia chose to include in her story the complete life and times of her mother Veronica, who in her later years due to the devasting effects of dementia and a stroke went to live in Antigua under her care. Dolvis later life path took a different journey as she chose to return to Jamaica while still young in her mid-fifties. Dolvis life in Jamaica took on another dimension as she became busy in her new life taking on many roles in Jamaica and starting many projects and businesses while in Jamaica. These include a realtor agent for her friends in Canada, giving extensively to her church such as buying and donating a bus. Also creating a charity for orphan children in need, running a guest home, and creating a tuck shop at her place of employment. As a result, Dolvis new life in Jamaica will be given the attention it deserves in my second book which will be entitled "Returning Residents & their Contributions to Island Life".

It is our hope that this book will inspire you and give you the courage to find your own life path and to embrace the struggles with less fear and full of hope. Embracing the knowledge that others have gone before and have succeeded. It is our wish that their spirit will provide that guiding light, constantly breathing new life and encouragement as you venture out and battle whatever obstacles you might face along the way. It is our prayer that this book and our story will continue to live and breathe because of your challenges and because of what you will accomplish through those struggles. Our hope is that they will live through you as angels to guide your path, directing you and keeping you strong to the end. Continue to fight to live your dream. BE BLESSED AS DOLVIS AND VERONICA CONTINUE TO WATCH OVER US!!

CREATION OF DOVE KRIB

DOVE KRIB has been created in memory of our mothers to encourage arts in young people. Fifteen percent of all sales will go towards DOVE KRIB TO support Afro-Caribbean artists especially in the area of writing which includes books, poetry and essays. Both Dolvis and Veronica had a passion for helping others from young to old in improving their conditions in life. We will endeavour to use these funds to support education in the arts, scholarships and competitions that will highlight and bring about cultural awareness and provide a continued legacy for the black community.

STUDY GROUP GUIDE QUESTIONS

|||||||||||||||||||||||||||||||||||||||||||||||||||||||||||||||||||||||||||||||||||||||||||||

1. What are your thoughts on the early life of Veronica and Dolvis in their native countries?
2. What are the similarities in their reason to leave their country to immigrate? What are the differences in their choices prior to immigrating?
3. Which one of the ladies choices can you most relate to and why?
4. What do you feel were some of the most difficult challenges these women faced in immigrating to Canada? Have you had similar challenges and how did you overcome those challenges?
5. Which of the women were you most sympathetic to and why?
6. Who did you most identify with and what are her strengths and weaknesses?
7. Imagine yourself as Dolvis or Veronica and how would you have dealt with the issue of unfaithfulness in your marriage?
8. What is your heritage and what are the strengths that you feel that heritage has brought to your development and growth?
9. What is the most important lesson or idea that you have been able to take from this book?
10. How do you know, feel that your heritage has prepared and strengthen you for your future goals in life?

CPSIA information can be obtained
at www.ICGtesting.com
Printed in the USA
BVHW030332020223
657591BV00001B/61